diet workshop's recipes for healthy living

diet workshop's recipes for healthy living

lois l. lindauer and sally sampson

doubleday new york london toronto sydney auckland

PUBLISHED BY DOUBLEDAY

a division of Bantam Doubleday Dell Publishing Group, Inc.

1540 Broadway, New York, New York 10036

DOUBLEDAY and the portrayal of an anchor with a dolphin are
trademarks of Doubleday, a division of Bantam Doubleday Dell
Publishing Group, Inc.

Nutritional analyses have been compiled with the use of ESHA software,
The Food Processor Plus® Version 5.0.

Book design and ornamentation by Gretchen Achilles

Library of Congress Cataloging-in-Publication Data

Lindauer, Lois Lyons.
   Diet Workshop's recipes for healthy living / Lois L. Lindauer
and Sally Sampson. — 1st ed.
      p.   cm.
   Includes index.
   1. Low-fat diet—Recipes.   1. Sampson, Sally, 1955–   . II. Diet
Workshop, Inc.   III. Title.
RM237.7.L56   1995
641.5'635—dc20   94-26401
                                                              CIP

ISBN 0-385-47251-X

10 9 8 7 6 5 4 3

This book is dedicated to the millions of people who like to eat food that tastes wonderful and permits them to remain thin and fit. Among those people are my husband, Bill Seltz, and my children and their spouses, Karen and Ross Herlands, Amy and Todd Eisenberg.

—lois l. lindauer

For Mark and Lauren, the biggest eaters of all.

—sally sampson

acknowledgments

My thanks to Darlene Hines, my assistant, and to Karen Beatty, who calculated all our nutritional analyses.

—lois l. lindauer

With thanks to everyone who came to endless dinners: you know who you are. And to Doe and Judy, who didn't come to dinner but should have.

—sally sampson

contents

chicken

beef, pork, and veal

drinks

index

foreword

Happiness may be wearing a size 6 dress, but an even greater happiness comes if you have had to work for it. Nothing beats the satisfaction of having accomplished the difficult goal of losing weight and adopting a pattern of healthy eating.

I am a person who had been fat all her life, from age five. When people ask what finally motivated me to lose my "baby fat" at age thirty-two, I tell them that for me weight loss was a matter of survival. The extra pounds I carried around weighed down my life.

I lost weight by following a simple plan. In the sixties, we weren't blessed with good-tasting low-calorie, low-fat cookies, cheeses, and mayonnaise; we didn't even have sugar replacements and diet drinks so easily available. I lost weight following a plan that provided me with food I could eat at any time of the day or night. I didn't have to be hungry. This was the key to my success. When I was overweight, a good part of my time was spent either thinking about food or eating it. I ate when I was unhappy. But I also ate when I was happy. Food was, and is, very important to me.

After my weight loss, I became an evangelist. I thought that if I could lose weight and keep it off, others could as well. I wanted to help others have the same feelings of satisfaction I had achieved, and in 1965 my zeal and enthusiasm prompted me to start Diet Workshop. From the beginning, we recognized the value of, and followed, a low-fat diet plan patterned after Dr. Norman Jolliffe's Prudent Diet. Dr. Jollife, Director of the Bureau of Nutrition for the New York City Department of Health during the 1950s and early 1960s, developed the first diet based upon a well-balanced eating plan. From day one, we gave people nutrition information and an exercise program. We offered the group format for inspiration and support, and each Diet Workshop class was always, and still is, led by someone who has successfully lost weight.

Currently, over two thousand DW groups in twelve states throughout the East and Midwest meet weekly to discuss their weight loss goals and support each other as only fellow dieters can. Our philosophy now, as it was in the beginning, rests on the three proven cornerstones of successful weight loss: nutrition, behavior change, and exercise.

When people ask me how I have managed to avoid regaining the weight, which is the norm, I tell them it's a combination of many factors, including perseverance, creativity, and motivation—the same as for the achievement of any goal.

Behind these simple words are thousands of hours of positive self-talk, hundreds of humbling experiences, and tens of hours spent in self-discovery.

Food is still very important to me. I like to eat healthy food, food that tastes good. Like creamy Carrot Soup with Roasted Chestnuts. Whole Roast Chicken with Butternut Squash and Pears. Overstuffed Blue Potatoes. Ricotta Cake with Hazelnuts and Lemon. Diet fare? Not at all. Yet these, and the other recipes in *Diet Workshop's Recipes for Healthy Living*, are healthy, low in calories and fat, and all of them taste great. That's where the creativity comes in! What we are doing in this book is giving you satisfying alternatives to the high-fat, calorie-rich food being offered all around you. And best of all, this book has something for everyone: dieters who want ideas for creative meals; people who have successfully lost weight and need to know how to maintain the loss; those who simply want to eat well but don't know how to prepare interesting meals.

While there is some information here that will help you with breakfast and lunch, we've chosen to focus on dinner. Recipes and chapters are organized by main ingredients and include dishes reflecting many styles and cuisines, including Chinese, Mexican, and classic Italian, and employing such cooking methods as grilling, steaming, and roasting. But what the recipes have in common is that they all contain less than 25 percent fat, a fact you'll find more amazing with each dish you prepare and eat.

With *Diet Workshop's Recipes for Healthy Living*, you have in hand the tool you need for eating well with enjoyment. All you have to supply is the desire. So if you like to eat well, and who doesn't, *Diet Workshop's Recipes for Healthy Living* can provide the rest. *Bon appétit, à votre santé.*

—lois l. lindauer

setting up a pantry

There is no mystery to setting up a pantry and also being sensitive to calories and fats. Your pantry can contain, and you can eat, just about anything; you just have to learn to use the pantry's contents. And our intention in this book is to teach you those secrets.

dried herbs and spices

All spices are not created equal. A jar of oregano you bought four years ago is not going to have the same kick as one recently purchased. This will make a huge difference in the taste of your cooking. The best dried herbs and spices we have found are packed by Dean & DeLuca (560 Broadway, New York, New York 10012, 1-800-221-7714) in New York City. Their spices are packed in tins and are, therefore, not affected by light, so they have a stronger flavor and a longer shelf life. They are available by mail order and are sold in many specialty stores around the country. The following list does not encompass their entire line, which is huge, but is what we consider essential for the preparation of the recipes in this book.

Basil

Bay leaves

Cardamom, ground

Cayenne pepper

Chili powder

Cinnamon, ground

Cumin, ground

Curry powder

Fennel seeds

Ginger, ground

Marjoram

Nutmeg, ground

Oregano, Greek

Paprika

Pepper: red flakes, black, white

Rosemary

Sesame seeds

Tarragon

Thyme

dry goods
(available in supermarkets and specialty food stores)

Artichoke bottoms, in water

Artichoke hearts, in water

Baking powder

Baking soda

Beans, canned: red kidney, white cannellini, black turtle

Beans, dried: red kidney, white cannellini, black turtle, lentil

Bouillon cubes: low-sodium chicken and vegetable

Broths: low-sodium chicken and vegetable

Chutney: assorted kinds

Flour: unbleached, all-purpose white

Milk, nonfat dry

Mushrooms, dried: shiitake

Mustards, Dijon: whole grain, flavored

Pasta, dried: various shapes and sizes

Rice: white, brown, Arborio

Salt, kosher and table

Soy sauce: light and dark

Sugars: white and brown and substitutes

Sun-dried tomatoes: dried and paste

Tomatoes, whole plum: chopped, paste

Tuna, packed in water

Vinegars: balsamic, white wine, red wine

Wines: dry white and red

refrigerator

Cheese, Parmesan

Milk, skim

Yogurt, plain: nonfat and low-fat

fruits and vegetables

Apples

Carrots

Celery

Garlic

Gingerroot

Lemons

Limes

Potatoes, red and baking

Red onions

Shallots

Spanish onions

Tomatoes

freezer

Cut-up chicken

Assorted frozen fruit (raspberries, strawberries, bananas)

equipping a kitchen

The following list of equipment is certainly not essential but it will help with the recipes in this book and most others. In most cases, we do not recommend brands and do so only when we feel it really makes a difference. A word about pots and pans. We strongly recommend both Calphalon and Berndes nonstick cookware. These brands are unequaled; they are heavy-bottomed and heat evenly; they brown meat beautifully, are easy to clean, and should last a lifetime. The prices are relatively high but we feel that use of high-quality cookware will make a huge difference in your cooking and in this area, it makes more sense to buy the best and buy once. If these brands are not available locally, they can be purchased through the Crate and Barrel catalog (1-800-323-5461) and the Williams Sonoma catalog (1-800-541-2233).

Food processor (we recommend Cuisinart)

Blender (we recommend Oster)

Heavy-bottomed 6- or 8-quart stockpot with lid (for a stockpot, it is not necessary to purchase nonstick)

2-quart saucepan, nonstick

3-quart saucepan, nonstick

1 shallow roasting pan, 15 × 10 × 2, nonstick

8-inch skillet or sauté pan, nonstick

10-inch skillet or sauté pan, nonstick

8-inch cast-iron skillet

Deep roasting pan with rack, 16 × 11 × 5

Jelly roll pan or baking sheet, 18 × 12 × 1, nonstick

Barbecue grill or hibachi

Wok

Assorted mixing bowls

Assorted ladles: 4-ounce, 6-ounce

Assorted wooden spoons

Measuring cups

Measuring spoons

Meat thermometer

Oven thermometer

Assorted spatulas, wood, rubber, and metal

Assorted wooden spoons

Slotted spoon

Stainless steel colander

Vegetable peeler

Poultry shears

Pepper grinder

Salad spinner

knives

As with cookware, the quality of your knives is important and will make a big difference in the ease with which you cook. Sabatier, Wustof, and Henckels are among the best.

Get your knives professionally sharpened at least once a year and sharpen, as needed, with a steel. Most specialty knife stores will do this for a minimal price.

Paring knives

6-inch cook's knife

8-inch chef's knife

10-inch carving knife

8-inch serrated bread knife

Sharpening steel

amounts and equivalents

In general, all the recipes call for whole heads, bunches, or very clear portions of vegetables. However, some people will want to know equivalents in pounds and/or in cups. But don't worry about being too exact. If your bunch of asparagus is just under a pound, or less than 3 cups, don't feel you must run out and buy more.

Asparagus: I pound = 3–3$\frac{1}{2}$ cups trimmed, peeled and chopped

Beans, fresh: I pound = 4 cups

Beets: I pound = about 5–6 trimmed beets

Broccoli: I average head = 1$\frac{1}{2}$–1$\frac{3}{4}$ pounds = 4$\frac{1}{2}$–5 cups chopped

Butternut squash: I large = 2–2$\frac{1}{2}$ pounds = 5 cups chopped

Cabbage: I medium head = 9–10 cups uncooked or 5$\frac{1}{2}$ cups cooked

Carrot: I medium = $\frac{1}{6}$ pound = $\frac{3}{4}$ cup chopped

Celery: I bunch = 1$\frac{3}{4}$–2 pounds = 12–14 stalks

Cucumber: I medium = $\frac{1}{2}$ pound

Eggplant: I medium = 1$\frac{1}{2}$ pounds = 6 cups diced

Endive: I medium = $\frac{1}{2}$ pound = I cup sliced

Fennel: I pound = about 2$\frac{1}{2}$ cups chopped

Garlic: I clove = I teaspoon chopped

Leeks: I average bunch = 4–5 leeks

Mushrooms: I pound = 6–7 cups trimmed and sliced

Pepper: I medium = $\frac{1}{3}$ pound

Potato: I medium or 4 small = $\frac{1}{2}$ pound = 2 cups diced

Spanish onion: I large = 1$\frac{1}{2}$–2 cups chopped

Spinach: I pound = 8–9 cups chopped

Summer squash: I medium = $\frac{1}{2}$ pound

Sweet potato: I medium = $\frac{1}{2}$–$\frac{3}{4}$ pound = 2–2$\frac{1}{2}$ cups diced

Tomato: I medium = $\frac{1}{3}$ pound

Turnips: I pound = 4 cups chopped

Watercress: I pound = 3$\frac{1}{2}$ cups chopped

Zucchini: I medium = $\frac{1}{2}$ pound = 1$\frac{3}{4}$ cups sliced

the basics

vegetable stock

Indispensable for soup-making, a good vegetable stock also makes a tasty alternative for "sautéing" and steaming. This stock is flavorful enough to stand on its own.

yield: about 8 cups

2 large leeks, including greens, roots discarded

3 carrots, sliced

2 stalks celery, sliced

3 Idaho potatoes, sliced

8 sprigs parsley

4 garlic cloves, peeled

4 sun-dried tomatoes

2 bay leaves

12 black peppercorns

8 cups cold water

1 teaspoon kosher salt or more, to taste

Quarter leeks lengthwise and thinly slice. Wash leeks by soaking them in several changes of water. Be careful to get rid of all the sand.

Combine all the ingredients, except the salt, in a 6- or 8-quart stockpot and bring to a boil over high heat. Reduce heat to low, partially cover, and simmer for 1 hour, stirring occasionally.

Strain soup and discard vegetables and bay leaves. Return soup to soup pot if reheating immediately (or pour into container if storing) and add salt to taste.

Refrigerate until ready to use. The stock can also be stored in the freezer for up to 4 months.

per 1-cup serving

Calories	38.4	Cholesterol	0 mg
Protein	4.8 g	Calcium	9.6 mg
Carbohydrates	.96 g	Iron	.504 mg
Fat—Total	1.44 g	Sodium	72 mg

chicken stock

Although there are some terrific prepared chicken stocks on the market, there is really no substitute for the taste and aroma of homemade stock. Cook and serve it the day you make it, or freeze it to use up to 4 weeks later.

yield: about 10 cups

Carcass and neck from 1 (6–7 pound) stewing chicken

2 stalks celery, cut in half

1 parsnip, cut in half

3 carrots, cut in half

1 small bunch leeks, including greens, root discarded

2 bay leaves

1 teaspoon dried thyme

8 cups water

1 teaspoon kosher salt

Quarter leeks lengthwise and thinly slice. Wash leeks by soaking them in several changes of water. Be careful to get rid of all the sand.

Combine all ingredients except for salt in a 6- or 8-quart stockpot and add about 8 cups cold water, or enough to cover. Cook over medium heat until it comes to a slow boil. Reduce heat to low and cook for 3 hours.

Strain stock. Discard carcass, vegetables, and bay leaves. Refrigerate stock and when it has completely cooled, skim off and discard the congealed fat. Add salt to taste.

per 1-cup serving

Calories	38.4	Cholesterol	0 mg
Protein	4.8 g	Calcium	9.6 mg
Carbohydrates	.96 g	Iron	.504 mg
Fat—Total	1.44 g	Sodium	72 mg

yogurt cheese

Yogurt Cheese is simply thickened yogurt, a marvelous alternative to sour cream or cream cheese in any recipe. You may use either nonfat or low-fat yogurt. If you use nonfat, the calories will be only 47 per serving and the fat less than 1 gram.

yield: about 1 $^1/_4$ cups

1 quart nonfat or low-fat plain yogurt

Line a colander with cheesecloth or muslin. Place colander over a large bowl.

Place yogurt in colander, cover and refrigerate, covered, overnight.

Discard the liquid that has drained into the bowl. Yogurt cheese keeps 4 days in refrigerator.

per $^1/_4$-cup serving (using low-fat yogurt)

Calories	60.6	Cholesterol	6.3 mg
Protein	5.9 g	Calcium	195 mg
Carbohydrates	5.3 g	Iron	.058 mg
Fat—Total	1.64 g	Sodium	50.6 mg

roasted garlic

Versatile roasted garlic serves as an unusual accompaniment to vegetables or roast chicken or as a spread on crackers or toast. It is not only easy to make, it also lasts well in the refrigerator.

makes 2 servings

1 head garlic

$1/8$ teaspoon kosher salt

$1/4$ cup Vegetable or Chicken Stock (page 17 or 18) or low-sodium canned or from bouillon cube

Preheat oven to 450 degrees.

Being careful to keep the garlic head intact, remove as much of the paper as you can. Place on a large piece of aluminum foil and sprinkle with salt. Sprinkle with chicken stock and seal by folding up the edges of the foil to make a packet.

Bake for about 45 minutes or until garlic is soft and tender. When cool enough to handle, remove remaining peel and, if using as a puree, mash with a fork.

per serving

Calories	26.9	Cholesterol	0 mg
Protein	1.14 g	Calcium	32.6 mg
Carbohydrates	5.95 g	Iron	.306 mg
Fat—Total	.09 g	Sodium	3.06 mg

roasted peppers

Like roasted garlic, roasted peppers are a staple of the adventurous cook. Added to turkey or tuna to jazz up a sandwich or pureed over pasta, they add an exotic touch. Roasted peppers can be broiled or roasted, as you prefer.

Red, yellow, or green bell peppers

Preheat broiler or oven to 400 degrees.

Place pepper(s) directly under the broiler, as close together as possible. Blacken peppers on all sides. Remove peppers and place in a heavy plastic or paper bag and let sweat for about 10 minutes. Remove burned skin, then seed and stem peppers.

per pepper

Calories	30.1	Cholesterol	0 mg
Protein	1.07 g	Calcium	11.3 mg
Carbohydrates	7.11 g	Iron	.512 mg
Fat—Total	.224 g	Sodium	2.23 mg

caramelized onions

Cooking onions for a long time over very low heat gives them a sweetness and smoothness. Try these as is for a tasty side dish or smothering a turkey burger.

yield: about 1 cup

1 teaspoon olive oil

1 Spanish onion, peeled and thinly sliced

2 tablespoons balsamic vinegar

1 teaspoon brown sugar or brown sugar substitute

Salt to taste

Heat a large skillet over medium-high flame and add oil. Add onion. Cook over low heat for about 45 minutes or until onion starts to brown, stirring occasionally.

Raise heat to high and gradually stir in vinegar and brown sugar. Salt to taste.

per ¼-cup serving

Calories	27.5	Cholesterol	0 mg
Protein	.416 g	Calcium	8.28 mg
Carbohydrates	4.28 g	Iron	.143 mg
Fat—Total	1.18 g	Sodium	1.45 mg

diet workshop's recipes for healthy living

tomato salsa

Versatile tomato salsa may accompany simple chicken, pork, or beef dishes, be eaten alone, or mixed with yogurt for a dip with pizzazz.

yield: about 3 cups

4 fresh tomatoes, cored and coarsely chopped

1 red onion, peeled and coarsely chopped

2 garlic cloves, peeled and chopped

1 green or yellow bell pepper, coarsely chopped

$1/4$ cup finely chopped fresh cilantro (see headnote, page 74)

$1/4$ teaspoon cayenne pepper

$1/4$ teaspoon salt

1 tablespoon fresh lime juice

Combine all ingredients in a large bowl. Cover and refrigerate at least 4 hours or overnight.

per $1/2$-cup serving

Calories	29.3	Cholesterol	0 mg
Protein	1.13 g	Calcium	12.7 mg
Carbohydrates	6.57 g	Iron	.531 mg
Fat—Total	.365 g	Sodium	97.2 mg

soups

gazpacho

Delicious as the first course of a light summer dinner or a main course for lunch, gazpacho is a delightful way to show off summer's bounty. If you want a finer soup, either chop the vegetables smaller or puree half the gazpacho in a food processor. If you prefer, substitute fresh dill or cilantro for the basil.

yield: about 9 cups

1/2 red onion, peeled and coarsely chopped

2 fresh tomatoes, cored and coarsely chopped

2 cucumbers, peeled, seeded, and diced

2 yellow, red, or green bell peppers, seeded and diced

2 cups low-sodium tomato juice

1/2–3/4 cup red wine vinegar

1/2 teaspoon salt

1/2 teaspoon black pepper

1/4 cup coarsely chopped fresh basil

Combine all ingredients in a large mixing bowl and refrigerate, covered, for at least 4 hours.

per 1-cup serving

Calories	36	Cholesterol	0 mg
Protein	1.5 g	Calcium	23.4 mg
Carbohydrates	8.62 g	Iron	.92 mg
Fat—Total	.296 g	Sodium	129 mg

vichyssoise

By replacing the traditional heavy cream with evaporated skim milk, you eliminate virtually all of the fat and none of the flavor. Although classic vichyssoise is served chilled, this one works hot as well.

yield: about 9 cups

1 bunch leeks, including greens, roots discarded

5$^1/_4$ cups Chicken Stock (page 18) or low-sodium canned or from bouillon cubes

4 medium red new potatoes, peeled, if desired

$^3/_4$ cup evaporated skim milk

$^1/_2$ teaspoon ground nutmeg

$^1/_4$ teaspoon black pepper

Quarter leeks lengthwise and thinly slice. Wash leeks by soaking them in several changes of water. Be careful to get rid of all the sand.

Combine leeks and $^1/_4$ cup chicken stock in a heavy-bottomed 6- or 8-quart stockpot and bring to a boil over high heat. Reduce heat to medium low and cook about 15 minutes or until the leeks have wilted.

Add potatoes and remaining chicken stock. Cover and return to the boil. Reduce heat to low and cook, uncovered, for about 20 minutes or until the potatoes are tender.

Place solids in a food processor. Process until completely smooth, gradually adding broth. Transfer to a bowl as processed. Add any remaining broth, the skim milk, nutmeg, and pepper. If serving hot, return to soup pot, reheat, and serve immediately. If serving cold, cover and refrigerate at least 2 hours or overnight.

per 1-cup serving

Calories	116	Cholesterol	.765 mg
Protein	6.06 g	Calcium	96.2 mg
Carbohydrates	20.8 g	Iron	1.41 mg
Fat—Total	1.07 g	Sodium	77.7 mg

chilled curried tomato soup with cucumbers

A flavor-bursting mouthful, the cucumbers and yogurt cool you down while the curry heats you up.

yield: about 9 cups

$^1/_4$ cup fresh lemon juice (about 1 lemon)

1 (46-ounce) can low-sodium tomato juice

1$^1/_2$ tablespoons curry powder

$^1/_2$ cup chopped fresh parsley

$^1/_4$ cup red wine vinegar

1 cup nonfat buttermilk

2 cups nonfat plain yogurt

2 cucumbers, peeled, seeded, and thinly sliced

Place lemon juice, tomato juice, curry powder, parsley, vinegar, buttermilk, and yogurt in a food processor fitted with a steel blade or blender. Process until smooth. Stir in cucumbers by hand; do not use a blender or food processor. Cover and chill for at least 2 hours.

per 1-cup serving

Calories	80.2	Cholesterol	1.93 mg
Protein	5.76 g	Calcium	172 mg
Carbohydrates	14.9 g	Iron	1.58 mg
Fat—Total	.686 g	Sodium	87.6 mg

chilled borscht

2 large bunches beets, leaves and roots discarded, scrubbed clean

6 cups water or Chicken Stock (page 18) or low-sodium canned or from bouillon cubes

2 tablespoons fresh lemon juice

3 cups nonfat buttermilk

Salt and pepper to taste

1–2 tablespoons chopped fresh dill (optional)

1/2 bunch scallions, including greens, chopped (optional)

Yogurt (for garnish) (optional)

Combine beets and water or chicken stock in a heavy-bottomed 8-quart stockpot and bring to a boil over high heat. Reduce heat to low and cook, partially covered, for about 35 minutes or until the beets are tender. Set aside to cool to room temperature. Peel and slice thin.

Place beets in a blender or food processor fitted with a steel blade and process, gradually adding broth, lemon juice, and buttermilk, until smooth. Refrigerate for at least 2 hours.

Add salt and pepper to taste and garnish with dill, scallions, and yogurt, if desired.

per 1-cup serving

Calories	112	Cholesterol	3.22 mg
Protein	7.16 g	Calcium	136 mg
Carbohydrates	18.2 g	Iron	1.42 mg
Fat—Total	1.59 g	Sodium	230 mg

chilled strawberry soup

Although this is perfect with strawberries, feel free to experiment with mangoes, peaches, melons, or any combination of fruits.

yield: about 6 cups

3 cups fresh strawberries

2 cups nonfat buttermilk

2–3 tablespoons honey

1 teaspoon vanilla extract

garnish:

1 cup fresh blueberries

1 cup fresh raspberries

1 tablespoon plus 1 teaspoon chopped fresh mint

Place strawberries in the bowl of a food processor fitted with a steel blade and process until smooth. Gradually add buttermilk, honey, and vanilla. Place in a large serving bowl, cover, and refrigerate about 1 hour or until chilled. Garnish with whole berries and fresh mint.

per 1-cup serving

Calories	107	Cholesterol	2.86 mg
Protein	3.52 g	Dietary Fiber	3.39 g
Carbohydrates	22.3 g	Calcium	111 mg
Fat—Total	1.19 g	Sodium	88.2 mg

black bean soup

Low-fat black bean soup is a hearty meal in itself, complete in protein and carbohydrates.

yield: about 9 cups

1 pound black turtle beans plus water to cover beans

8 cups water, Vegetable or Chicken Stock (page 17 or 18) or low-sodium canned or from bouillon cubes

2 carrots, finely chopped

1 celery stalk, finely chopped

1 Spanish onion, peeled and finely chopped

2 bay leaves

1 teaspoon dried basil

1 teaspoon dried Greek oregano

1 teaspoon cayenne pepper or more, to taste

1 teaspoon ground cumin

2 tablespoons tomato paste

2 tablespoons red wine vinegar

Place black beans in an 8-quart stockpot and cover with water. Bring to a boil. Reduce heat to medium low and cook, partially covered, for about 2 hours or until soft. Add more water if necessary while cooking. Drain and rinse thoroughly.

Combine all ingredients, except red wine vinegar, in a heavy-bottomed 8-quart stockpot and cook over medium-high heat until the mixture begins to boil.

Reduce heat to medium low and cook, partially covered, for 4–5 hours or until soup has halved in volume and is very thick. Add vinegar and remove bay leaves just prior to serving.

per 1-cup serving

Calories	116	Cholesterol	0 mg
Protein	9.2 g	Calcium	32.1 mg
Carbohydrates	16.5 g	Iron	1.76 mg
Fat—Total	1.64 g	Sodium	103 mg

chinese chicken soup

Traditional chicken soup with an oriental touch.

yield: about 10 cups

3/4 pound boneless and skinless chicken breasts

8 cups Chicken Stock (page 18) or low-sodium canned or from bouillon cubes

1 quarter-size slice fresh gingerroot, peeled, if desired

4 garlic cloves, peeled and pressed or finely chopped

2 carrots, sliced

2 celery stalks, peeled and thinly sliced

1/2 cup long grain white rice

1 tablespoon soy sauce

2 tablespoons Japanese rice vinegar

1 bunch scallions, including greens, thinly sliced

Place chicken breasts in a single layer in a large skillet or sauté pan. Cover with 4 cups of the chicken stock and bring to a low boil over medium heat. Reduce heat to low and cook for about 10 minutes or until the breasts are cooked. When cool enough to handle, shred into bite-size pieces. Reserve chicken stock.

Place gingerroot, garlic cloves, carrots, celery, and remaining chicken stock in a heavy-bottomed 8-quart stockpot and bring to a boil over high heat. Reduce heat to low and cook for about 20 minutes or until vegetables are tender.

Add rice, reserved chicken and chicken stock, cover and cook for about 20 minutes or until rice is cooked. Add soy sauce, rice vinegar, and scallions and serve immediately.

per 1-cup serving

Calories	108	Cholesterol	21.8 mg
Protein	8.69 g	Calcium	20.6 mg
Carbohydrates	10.3 g	Iron	.953 mg
Fat—Total	3.4 g	Sodium	145 mg

spinach and white bean soup

Thick and satisfying, spinach and white bean soup serves up flavor, protein, and vegetables. Crusty bread and tomato salad complete it to make a perfect meal.

yield: about 10 cups

8$^{1}/_{2}$ cups Chicken or Vegetable Stock (page 18 or 17) or low-sodium canned or from bouillon cubes

1 Spanish onion, peeled and chopped

3 garlic cloves, peeled and chopped or crushed

2 celery stalks, peeled and sliced

2 carrots, diced

2$^{1}/_{2}$ cups cooked white beans (about 1$^{1}/_{2}$ cups dried; see Note)

3 cups packed roughly chopped spinach leaves

4–5 canned or fresh plum tomatoes, roughly chopped

1 cup small pasta, such as orzo or alphabets

1 tablespoon chopped fresh basil

Combine $^{1}/_{2}$ cup stock, onion, garlic, celery, and carrots in a heavy-bottomed 6- or 8-quart stockpot and cook over medium-low heat about 15 minutes or until vegetables are tender. Add remaining stock and white beans and bring to a low boil. Reduce heat to low and cook, partially covered, for 1 hour.

Add spinach and tomatoes and cook for 10 minutes. In a separate pot, just prior to serving, cook pasta. Drain pasta and add to soup. Just before serving, add fresh basil.

NOTE:

I pound (2$^1/4$ cups) dried beans equals about 6 cups cooked or canned, or about 3$^1/2$ sixteen-ounce cans.

To quick-cook dried beans, rinse, then place in a large stockpot and add enough water to cover by about 2 to 4 inches. Bring to a boil over high heat, reduce heat to low, partially cover, and simmer gently for 1–2 hours, adding more water if necessary, until beans are soft. Discard the cooking liquid and proceed with recipe.

per 1-cup serving

Calories	158	Cholesterol	0 mg
Protein	10.6 g	Calcium	71.9 mg
Carbohydrates	25.1 g	Iron	2.84 mg
Fat—Total	1.89 g	Sodium	91.1 mg

double mushroom soup

The addition of shiitake mushrooms to traditional mushroom soup creates a beefy, lush flavor. Eat as is or strain and use as a stock when you want something richer than water or Chicken Stock.

yield: about 8 cups

5¼ cups Chicken or Vegetable Stock (page 18 or 17) or low-sodium canned or from bouillon cubes

1 Spanish onion, peeled and finely chopped

1 teaspoon dried rosemary

1 pound white button mushrooms, coarsely chopped

8 fresh shiitake mushrooms, coarsely chopped (see Note)

Combine ¼ cup stock and onion in a heavy-bottomed 4- or 6-quart stockpot and cook over medium heat about 15 minutes or until onion is translucent.

Add rosemary, mushrooms, and remaining stock and bring to a boil. Reduce heat to low and cook, partially covered, for 1 hour.

Serve as is, or, if a smooth soup is desired, puree.

NOTE:

If fresh shiitake mushrooms are not available, use an equivalent amount of dried shiitake mushrooms instead. Before adding to soup, soak in 1 cup hot water for 20 minutes and drain. Reserve water and substitute 1 cup mushroom broth for 1 cup stock in recipe).

per 1-cup serving

Calories	55.7	Cholesterol	0 mg
Protein	4.85 g	Calcium	12.3 mg
Carbohydrates	7.28 g	Iron	1.13 mg
Fat—Total	1.24 g	Sodium	50.4 mg

smoky broccoli vegetable soup

Not even the most sophisticated chef will guess the elusive ingredients in this distinctive soup. For a soup with virtually no calories or fat, omit the turkey breast.

yield: about 10 cups

6 cups Chicken or Vegetable Stock (page 18 or 17) or low-sodium canned or from bouillon cubes

2 shallots or 1 small onion, peeled and sliced

1 carrot, sliced

1 celery stalk, peeled and sliced

2 medium-size zucchini, sliced

1 small head broccoli, stems peeled and julienned, florets chopped

1 tomato, cored and diced

$^1/_8$ pound cooked smoked turkey breast, diced

Yogurt Cheese (page 19) (for garnish)

Combine $^1/_2$ cup stock, shallots, carrot, celery, and zucchini in a heavy-bottomed 6- or 8-quart stockpot and cook over low heat for about 15 minutes or until the vegetables are soft.

Add broccoli stems, remaining stock, and tomato and bring to a boil over high heat. Reduce heat to low and cook about 20 minutes or until the broccoli is tender.

Remove solids and place in the bowl of a food processor fitted with a steel blade or a blender. Process until smooth, gradually adding remaining broth. Return pureed soup to pot. Add smoked turkey and broccoli florets. Cook until just heated through.

Serve garnished with a dollop of yogurt cheese.

per 1-cup serving

Calories	46.8	Cholesterol	2.32 mg
Protein	5.27 g	Calcium	24.1 mg
Carbohydrates	4.3 g	Iron	.712 mg
Fat—Total	1.12 g	Sodium	137 mg

chicken and shiitake mushroom soup

Grandma's specialty takes an unusual turn. If you are using canned stock, find one that is salt-free if possible. Remember, it's always easy to add salt, but not so easy to get rid of it.

yield: about 12 cups

11 cups Chicken Stock (page 18) or low-sodium canned or from bouillon cubes

1 small yellow onion or 1/2 large Spanish onion, peeled and chopped

2–3 carrots, diced

1 large celery stalk, peeled and diced

8 fresh shiitake mushrooms, stems removed and sliced (see Note, page 36)

1/3 cup pearl barley

1 cup dry white wine

1 bay leaf

2 teaspoons dried basil

1 pound boneless and skinless chicken breasts

1/2 cup chopped fresh basil

Combine 1/2 cup stock, onion, carrots, and celery in a heavy-bottomed 6- or 8-quart stockpot and cook over low heat for about 15 minutes or until vegetables are tender.

Add mushrooms, barley, remaining chicken stock, white wine, bay leaf, and dried basil and cook over medium heat for 2 hours.

Poach chicken breasts by submerging them in the soup and letting them cook for about 10 minutes or until cooked through. Remove from soup, cool and shred.

Return chicken to soup, remove bay leaf, and add fresh basil just prior to serving.

per 1-cup serving

Calories	149	Cholesterol	24.2 mg
Protein	13.5 g	Calcium	26 mg
Carbohydrates	8.88 g	Iron	1.19 mg
Fat—Total	5.01 g	Sodium	100 mg

diet workshop's recipes for healthy living

minestrone i

Both these versions of hearty minestrone are light and delicious. Minestrone makes a great first course, main course, or an afternoon snack. Vary your flavors by substituting whatever fresh vegetables you have on hand.

yield: about 12 cups

10½ cups Chicken or Vegetable Stock (page 18 or 17) or low-sodium canned or from bouillon cubes

1 red onion, peeled and chopped

1 shallot, peeled and chopped

6 garlic cloves, peeled and chopped or crushed

3 carrots, halved and sliced

3 stalks celery, peeled and sliced

1 (16-ounce) can kidney beans, drained and rinsed

1 (16-ounce) can diced tomatoes, including liquid

2 bay leaves

1 teaspoon dried thyme

1 bunch kale, chopped

1 cup small dried pasta, such as elbows

Combine ½ cup stock, onion, shallot, garlic, carrots, and celery in a heavy-bottomed 6- or 8-quart stockpot and cook over medium heat for about 10 minutes or until the vegetables are translucent. Add beans, tomatoes, bay leaves, thyme, and kale and bring to a boil.

Reduce heat to low and cook, partially covered, for 2 hours. In a separate pot, cook pasta. Drain, and just prior to serving, ladle pasta into soup bowls. Remove the bay leaves before covering the pasta with the soup.

per 1-cup serving

Calories	128	Cholesterol	0 mg
Protein	8.74 g	Calcium	46.3 mg
Carbohydrates	19.5 g	Iron	2.11 mg
Fat—Total	1.73 g	Sodium	143 mg

minestrone ii

$^1/_2$ cup dried white beans, cleaned and picked over for pebbles (see Note, page 35)

2 quarts cold water

8$^1/_2$ cups Vegetable or Chicken Stock (page 17 or 18) or low-sodium canned
or from bouillon cubes

1 Spanish onion, peeled and finely chopped

2 garlic cloves, peeled and pressed or finely chopped

1 stalk celery, peeled and diced

1 potato, cubed

1 parsnip, diced

1–2 tablespoons dried basil

1 teaspoon dried marjoram

2 bay leaves

4 whole sun-dried tomatoes, finely chopped

1 medium-size zucchini, quartered lengthwise and sliced

1 medium-size yellow squash, quartered lengthwise and sliced

1 (28-ounce) can whole tomatoes, chopped, including liquid

$^1/_2$ cup orzo or any kind of small pasta, such as elbows

Chopped fresh parsley (for garnish)

Chopped fresh basil (for garnish)

Grated Asiago cheese (for garnish)

Combine white beans and water in medium heavy-bottomed stockpot and bring to a boil over high heat. Reduce heat to low and simmer, partially covered, for about 1 hour. When beans are soft, rinse with cold water, drain, and add to soup.

While beans are simmering, combine ½ cup stock, onion, garlic, celery, potato, and parsnip in a heavy-bottomed 6- or 8-quart soup pot, over high heat, and bring to a boil. Reduce heat to low and cook about 15 minutes or until onions are transparent.

Add dried herbs, sun-dried tomatoes, zucchini, and squash and cook for 10 minutes.

Add tomatoes and remaining stock and bring to a boil over high heat. Reduce heat to low and cook, partially covered, for 1–1½ hours, adding the beans when they are ready.

Just before you are ready to serve soup, bring it to a boil over high heat and add orzo. Reduce heat to medium and cook about 10 minutes or until orzo is done. Remove bay leaves before serving. If you are using pasta that is larger than orzo, cook it in a separate pot and add just prior to serving. Garnish with fresh herbs and Asiago cheese.

per 1-cup serving

Calories	116	Cholesterol	0 mg
Protein	7.05 g	Calcium	51.4 mg
Carbohydrates	19.7 g	Iron	2.04 mg
Fat—Total	1.4 g	Sodium	94.7 mg

butternut squash soup with sage

This soup is smooth and silky. Serve it as a first course for a grilled pork or chicken dinner. If you're not a butternut squash fan, don't turn the page: substitute any type of squash in this recipe or use carrots instead.

yield: about 10 cups

8¼ cups Chicken or Vegetable Stock (page 18 or 17) or low-sodium canned or from bouillon cubes

1 small Spanish onion, peeled and chopped

1 large butternut squash, peeled, seeded, and cubed (about 5–6 cups)

1 pear, cored and sliced

2 teaspoons dried sage

4 leaves fresh sage (for garnish)

Grated Parmesan cheese (for garnish)

Combine ¼ cup stock and Spanish onion in a heavy-bottomed 6- or 8-quart stockpot and cook over medium heat for about 15 minutes or until the onion is transparent.

Add butternut squash, pear, remaining stock, and dried sage and bring to a boil. Reduce heat to low and cook, covered, about 20 minutes or until the squash is tender.

Remove solids and place in a food processor fitted with a steel blade or a blender. Process until smooth, gradually adding remaining broth.

Garnish with fresh sage and grated Parmesan cheese.

per 1-cup serving

Calories	86.7	Cholesterol	0 mg
Protein	5.08 g	Calcium	54 mg
Carbohydrates	15 g	Iron	1.1 mg
Fat—Total	1.36 g	Sodium	63.8 mg

carrot soup with roasted chestnuts

Delicate carrot soup with chestnuts makes an elegant beginning for a chicken or fish dinner.

yield: about 10 cups

$^1/_2$ pound fresh chestnuts

7 cups Chicken or Vegetable Stock (page 18 or 17) or low-sodium canned or from bouillon cubes

1 small Spanish onion, peeled and chopped

1 pound carrots, sliced

1 celery stalk, peeled and sliced

1 quarter-size slice fresh gingerroot, peeled, if desired, and sliced

Preheat oven to 400 degrees.

Cut an X on the flat side of each chestnut. (It is critical that you X the chestnuts or they might burst.) Place in oven on a shallow pan and roast for 15 minutes.

Remove chestnuts from oven and rest until just cool enough to handle. Peel and set aside.

Put $^1/_4$ cup of the chicken stock and the onion in heavy-bottomed 8-quart stockpot and bring to a boil over high heat. Reduce heat to low and simmer about 15 minutes or until onion is translucent.

Add remaining ingredients, including chestnuts, and cook, over medium heat, about 25 minutes or until carrots are tender.

Remove solids and place in a food processor fitted with a steel blade or a blender. Process until smooth, gradually adding remaining broth.

per 1-cup serving

Calories	100	Cholesterol	0 mg
Protein	4.55 g	Calcium	29 mg
Carbohydrates	16.9 g	Iron	.853 mg
Fat—Total	1.64 g	Sodium	70.9 mg

sauces, dips

shiitake mushroom and tomato sauce

This flavorful, interesting sauce is hearty, rich, and best of all, virtually fat-free. It also makes a great topping for pizza.

yield: about 3 $^1/_2$ cups

$^1/_2$ cup red wine

3 garlic cloves, peeled and crushed or chopped

3 cups coarsely chopped fresh shiitake mushrooms

1 (28-ounce) can chopped tomatoes, including liquid

$^1/_2$ teaspoon black pepper

1 teaspoon dried Greek oregano

1 teaspoon dried basil

1 bay leaf

$^1/_4$ cup chopped fresh basil

Combine red wine, garlic, and shiitake mushrooms in a saucepan and cook over medium-low heat for about 15 minutes or until the mushrooms are soft.

Add tomatoes, pepper, and dried herbs and cook, partially covered, for 1–1½ hours.

Just prior to serving, remove the bay leaf and add the fresh basil.

per $^1/_2$-cup serving

Calories	71.3	Cholesterol	0 mg
Protein	2.18 g	Calcium	37.4 mg
Carbohydrates	14.5 g	Iron	1.11 mg
Fat—Total	.424 g	Sodium	188 mg

tomato sauce with sweet peppers and hot and sweet sausages

A healthy sauce made with sausage? Yes, thanks to turkey.

yield: 6^1/2–7 cups

4 sweet turkey sausages

4 spicy turkey sausages

1 Spanish onion, peeled and coarsely chopped

2 red bell peppers, seeded and diced

3 garlic cloves, peeled and chopped

2 (28-ounce) cans chopped tomatoes, including liquid

1 cup red wine

1 bay leaf

1 tablespoon dried Greek oregano

1 tablespoon dried basil

1 teaspoon dried fennel seeds

Crushed red pepper flakes to taste

Prick sausages all over with the tines of a fork. Place in a large skillet and cook over medium heat for about 20 minutes or until browned, turning occasionally. Set aside to cool.

In the same pan, cook onion, peppers, and garlic over medium heat until softened, adding water as necessary to prevent scorching. Add remaining ingredients, raise heat to high, and bring to a boil. Slice or chop reserved sausages and add to pot. Reduce heat to low and cook, partially covered, for 2 hours. Remove bay leaf before serving.

per ^{1}/2-cup serving

Calories	104	Cholesterol	21.7 mg
Protein	6.44 g	Calcium	40.2 mg
Carbohydrates	7.07 g	Iron	1.31 mg
Fat—Total	4.85 g	Sodium	436 mg

classic meat sauce

This recipe makes a ton of sauce but if you're going to go to all the trouble to make a low-fat version of this classic marinara sauce you might as well make enough to freeze for another meal. Of course, you can just as easily halve it.

yield: about 15 cups

1 red onion, peeled and coarsely chopped

1 Spanish onion, peeled and coarsely chopped

12 garlic cloves, peeled and chopped or crushed

1 cup water

2 pounds reduced-fat ground beef

3 (28-ounce) cans whole tomatoes, including juice, chopped

3 bay leaves

3 tablespoons dried Greek oregano

2 tablespoons dried basil

1 tablespoon fennel seeds

1 (6-ounce) can tomato paste

1 cup red wine

Combine onions, garlic, and 1 cup water in a heavy-bottomed 8-quart stockpot and cook, over medium-low heat, for about 15 minutes or until onion is translucent.

Crumble ground beef into the pan and cook for about 7 minutes or until it starts to lose its pinkness.

Add remaining ingredients and bring to a low boil over medium heat. Reduce heat to low and cook, partially covered, for 1½ hours. Remove bay leaves before serving.

per ½-cup serving

Calories	65.9	Cholesterol	0 mg
Protein	7.53 g	Calcium	27.1 mg
Carbohydrates	5.59 g	Iron	.728 mg
Fat—Total	1.33 g	Sodium	175 mg

barbecue sauce

This tangy barbecue sauce may be made up to 4 days ahead of time and stored in the refrigerator; it's great to have around to brush on chicken, fish, or beef when you want something special but don't have time to make anything complicated. Left chunky, it makes the world's best ketchup.

yield: about 4 cups

1 Spanish onion, peeled and coarsely chopped

1 red or yellow bell pepper, seeded and coarsely chopped

3–4 garlic cloves, peeled and chopped

2 tablespoons brown sugar

1 (28-ounce) can chunky-style tomatoes, including liquid

1–2 teaspoons black pepper

1 teaspoon chili powder

$1/4$ cup white vinegar

$1/4$ cup fresh lemon juice (about 1 lemon)

2 tablespoons Dijon mustard

1 cup tomato ketchup

$1/2$ cup water

$1/2$ teaspoon salt

Combine onion, pepper, garlic, and brown sugar in a large, heavy-bottomed saucepan and cook over very low heat for about 20 minutes or until the onion is caramelized. If the mixture appears to be in danger of scorching, add water, 1 tablespoon at a time.

Add all remaining ingredients and cook for 2 hours.

If you want a chunky sauce, leave as is. For a smooth one, remove half the sauce and place in a food processor fitted with a steel blade or a blender. Process until smooth. Repeat with remaining sauce.

per 1 tablespoon

Calories	9.51	Cholesterol	0 mg
Protein	.242 g	Calcium	5.53 mg
Carbohydrates	2.31 g	Iron	.136 mg
Fat—Total	.073 g	Sodium	88.6 mg

diet workshop's recipes for healthy living

chutney cream cheese

By using Yogurt Cheese, those who shun high-fat, high-cholesterol cream cheese can enjoy and serve rich, yet low-fat dips. Chutney cream cheese is wonderful stuffed inside celery stalks, tomatoes, even mushrooms, or you may serve it as a spread with pita triangles or as a dip with crudités.

yield: about $2^3/4$ cups

2 cups Yogurt Cheese (page 19)

1 cup mango chutney

1 teaspoon curry powder (optional)

Combine ingredients in a medium-size bowl and mix by hand until smooth.

per $^1/4$-cup serving

Calories	82.1	Cholesterol	4.58 mg
Protein	4.64 g	Calcium	151 mg
Carbohydrates	13.6 g	Iron	.395 mg
Fat—Total	1.32 g	Sodium	91.6 mg

herb cheese

Dip into herb cheese with toasted pita or a crudité or spread it on a turkey sandwich for a delightful taste surprise.

yield: about 1 cup

1 cup Yogurt Cheese (page 19)

¼ cup finely chopped fresh parsley

1–2 garlic cloves, peeled and finely chopped

1 tablespoon finely chopped fresh basil or 1 teaspoon dried basil

1 tablespoon finely chopped fresh oregano or 1 teaspoon dried oregano

2 teaspoons finely chopped fresh thyme or ⅔ teaspoon dried thyme

¼ teaspoon black pepper

¼ teaspoon salt

Combine ingredients in a medium-size bowl and mix by hand or blend, beat, or process until smooth.

per ¼-cup serving

Calories	64.2	Cholesterol	6.3 mg
Protein	6.11 g	Calcium	203 mg
Carbohydrates	6.03 g	Iron	.316 mg
Fat—Total	1.68 g	Sodium	186 mg

poached and smoked salmon spread

A holiday must, your guests will appreciate the luxe taste and the silky texture of this spread. Serve it with squares of brown bread and garnishes of minced red onion and capers.

yield: about 1 ¹/₂ cups

1 shallot, peeled

1 (8–12 ounce) fresh salmon fillet

1 cup low-sodium canned fish stock

¹/₂ pound smoked salmon, thinly sliced

Poach shallot and salmon fillet in fish stock for 8–10 minutes. Remove shallot and mash with fork. Blend in strips of smoked salmon. Add poached salmon and mash. Cover and refrigerate until ready to use. Serve chilled.

per 2 tablespoons

Calories	30.3	Cholesterol	8.69 mg
Protein	4.29 g	Calcium	3.32 mg
Carbohydrates	.25 g	Iron	.21 mg
Fat—Total	1.22 g	Sodium	82.4 mg

curried honey dip

Curried honey dip is tasty with fruits, especially pears and apples. It's also good with vegetables, crackers, and any kind of bread.

yield: about 1 ¹/₂ cups

¹/₂ cup honey

1–2 tablespoons curry powder

1 cup Yogurt Cheese (page 19)

Combine honey and curry powder in a small saucepan and heat until the honey is liquid. Remove from heat and cool to room temperature.

Add yogurt cheese, cover, and refrigerate at least 2 hours or overnight.

per 1 tablespoon

Calories	32.8	Cholesterol	1.05 mg
Protein	1.05 g	Calcium	34.8 mg
Carbohydrates	6.92 g	Iron	.156 mg
Fat—Total	.328 g	Sodium	8.92 mg

mustard dip

Sharp mustard dip makes a great contrast to raw or cooked vegetables and works as a wake-up flavor spread on sandwiches, as well.

yield: about 1 cup

1/2 cup dry mustard

3/4 cup white vinegar

1/2 cup dry white wine or dry vermouth

3 eggs

1/2 cup white sugar

1/2 tablespoon salt

Combine mustard, white vinegar, and white wine or vermouth in a small mixing bowl and let sit overnight.

The following morning, add eggs, sugar, and salt to the mustard mixture and beat until frothy. Place in a small saucepan and cook over medium-low heat, stirring occasionally, for 1 hour or until mixture starts to thicken. Cover and refrigerate until ready to use. Serve chilled.

per 1 tablespoon

Calories	43	Cholesterol	35.1 mg
Protein	1.04 g	Calcium	6.17 mg
Carbohydrates	7.03 g	Iron	.216 mg
Fat—Total	.825 g	Sodium	610 mg

onion dip

Lighter and tastier than the traditional onion dip, this version is heart healthy as well.

yield: about 1 cup

1 Caramelized Onion (page 22), chopped

³/₄ cup Yogurt Cheese (page 19)

¹/₂ teaspoon salt

¹/₂ teaspoon black pepper

Pinch cayenne pepper

Stir together all ingredients in a medium-size bowl. Cover and refrigerate for at least 2 hours or overnight.

per 1 tablespoon

Calories	18.2	Cholesterol	1.18 mg
Protein	1.21 g	Calcium	38.7 mg
Carbohydrates	2.06 g	Iron	.047 mg
Fat—Total	.604 g	Sodium	76.5 mg

roasted red pepper dip with cumin

The prototype of this dip was made with plenty of olive oil, but we discovered that even the most discerning critic could not tell the difference in either taste or texture when we substituted Yogurt Cheese for half the oil. You can serve it to guests with pita triangles, but it's also great with cold chicken and, for the adventurous, cold pasta.

yield: about 2 cups

1/2 Spanish onion, peeled and thinly sliced

2 garlic cloves, peeled

2 tablespoons water

I tablespoon brown sugar

3 roasted red bell peppers (page 21)

I tablespoon ground cumin

Juice of I lime

I tablespoon molasses

3 tablespoons Yogurt Cheese (page 19)

3 tablespoons chopped fresh parsley

Combine onion, garlic, and water in a small saucepan and cook over medium-low heat for about 10 minutes or until onion begins to soften. Add brown sugar and cook an additional 5 minutes.

Place contents of saucepan with all the other ingredients in a food processor fitted with a steel blade and blend until completely smooth. Cover and refrigerate until ready to use. Serve chilled.

per I tablespoon

Calories	7.64	Cholesterol	.148 mg
Protein	.251 g	Calcium	8.09 mg
Carbohydrates	1.69 g	Iron	.098 mg
Fat—Total	.061 g	Sodium	1.97 mg

fish

orange herb salmon

One of the staples of healthy eaters is fish, so we are always looking for tasty new ways to cook it. Having this recipe in your repertoire makes eating fish a great treat.

serves 4

marinade:

1 garlic clove, peeled and finely chopped or crushed

1 tablespoon finely chopped fresh cilantro (see headnote, page 74)

1/2 teaspoon grated orange peel

1/4 teaspoon ground cumin

1/4 teaspoon cayenne pepper

1/2 teaspoon dried Greek oregano

1/3 cup fresh orange juice

3 tablespoons fresh lime juice

1 1/2 pounds salmon fillets

Orange slices (for garnish)

Combine marinade ingredients in a medium-size glass or ceramic bowl and add salmon. Cover and refrigerate for no more than 2 hours, turning occasionally.

Prepare the grill or broiler. Remove salmon from marinade and reserve marinade. Cook salmon 3–5 minutes on each side, depending on thickness, or until fish flakes easily.

As the salmon is cooking, bring marinade to a boil over high heat and let cook 5 minutes. Serve on the side.

Garnish with fresh orange slices.

per serving

Calories	255	Cholesterol	93.6 mg
Protein	33.9 g	Calcium	25.3 mg
Carbohydrates	3.42 g	Iron	1.42 mg
Fat—Total	10.9 g	Sodium	75.3 mg

salmon fillet with raw tomato coulis

Any dieter knows that it can be a real trial to keep coming up with interesting healthy sauces for fish. The following sauce meets that challenge and, in addition to being wonderful with salmon, adds a new dimension to cod, halibut, or any fish of your choice.

serves 4

tomato coulis:

$1/4$ cup peeled and finely chopped red onion

2 garlic cloves, peeled and chopped or crushed

$1/4$ teaspoon dried thyme

$1/4$ teaspoon dried basil

$1/4$ teaspoon dried Greek oregano

2 tablespoons water

I large fresh tomato, coarsely chopped

2 teaspoons balsamic vinegar

2 teaspoons chopped fresh basil

I teaspoon chopped fresh oregano

$1 1/2$ pounds salmon fillet, in 4 pieces

Combine red onion, garlic, and dried herbs in a nonstick pan and cook over very low heat. As the mixture begins to look dry, add the water and deglaze the pan.

Cook for an additional 3 minutes or until the onion is soft. Remove from heat and add remaining ingredients. Set aside at room temperature or, if desired, refrigerate.

Prepare the grill or broiler. Cook the salmon fillets 3–5 minutes on each side, depending on thickness, or until fish flakes easily. Set aside to cool or serve immediately. Ladle a portion of the sauce onto each plate and top it with a serving of salmon.

per serving

Calories	255	Cholesterol	93.6 mg
Protein	34.2 g	Calcium	27.7 mg
Carbohydrates	3.16 g	Iron	1.61 mg
Fat—Total	11 g	Sodium	78.8 mg

fish

citrus salmon with ginger

There are two schools of thought about marinating. The first, and more common, is that the fish should be immersed in the marinade and allowed to sit for a few hours; then the marinade is poured off and the fish is cooked. The second is that the marinade should be treated as a sauce and poured over the cooked fish. This dish works both ways; see which you prefer.

serves 4

marinade:

1 orange

2 limes

1–2 tablespoons peeled, chopped fresh gingerroot

$^1/_2$ teaspoon cayenne pepper

2 scallions, including greens, sliced lengthwise

$1^1/_2$ pounds salmon fillet, skin on

Peel zest from orange and limes and reserve for garnish. Squeeze the fruits and combine the juices with the other marinade ingredients in a glass or ceramic bowl. Pour over salmon. Cover and refrigerate for no more than 2 hours.

Prepare the grill or broiler. Remove salmon from marinade, reserving marinade. Cook 3–5 minutes on each side, depending on thickness, or until the fish flakes easily.

While salmon is cooking, over high heat bring marinade to a boil in a small saucepan. Reduce heat to low and let cook 5 minutes. Serve on the side.

If you prefer, grill or broil salmon and pour marinade over each serving of salmon.

Garnish with slivers of orange and lime zest.

per serving

Calories	259	Cholesterol	93.6 mg
Protein	34 g	Calcium	25.5 mg
Carbohydrates	4.9 g	Iron	1.41 mg
Fat—Total	10.9 g	Sodium	75.3 mg

grilled softshell crabs with lemon and tarragon

Softshell crabs are only available fresh for a few months in the spring, so make the most of them. Prepare a few extra to serve cold in sandwiches the following day.

serves 4

marinade:

$1/3$ cup fresh lemon juice

$1/3$ cup Dijon mustard

2 tablespoons dried French tarragon

$1/4$ cup dry white wine

8–12 softshell crabs, depending on size

Combine marinade ingredients in a glass or ceramic bowl and pour over crabs. Cover and refrigerate no more than 2 hours.

Prepare grill. Place crabs on the grill and bring reserved marinade to a boil. Grill crabs 3 minutes on each side. To serve, pour marinade over crabs.

NOTE:

Instead of grilling the softshell crabs, try broiling or pan broiling (for about 3 minutes per side).

per serving

Calories	152	Cholesterol	120 mg
Protein	25.3 g	Calcium	145 mg
Carbohydrates	3.18 g	Iron	1.56 mg
Fat—Total	3.1 g	Sodium	594 mg

grilled softshell crabs with cilantro tequila dressing

dressing:

$^1/_2$ cup chopped fresh cilantro (see headnote, page 74)

$^1/_4$ teaspoon cayenne pepper

$^1/_2$ teaspoon chili powder

$^1/_2$ teaspoon ground cumin

1 garlic clove, peeled and pressed or finely chopped

Juice of 2 limes

2 tablespoons tequila

2 tablespoons low-fat mayonnaise

8–12 softshell crabs, depending on size

Prepare grill.

Prepare dressing by placing all ingredients in a food processor fitted with a steel blade. Process until completely incorporated. Set aside.

Place crabs on grill and grill for about 3 minutes on each side. Serve with dressing over them.

per serving

Calories	164	Cholesterol	122 mg
Protein	24.5 g	Calcium	129 mg
Carbohydrates	4.08 g	Iron	1.14 mg
Fat—Total	3.67 g	Sodium	375 mg

cajun catfish with fresh watercress sauce

Catfish are native to the waters of the Mississippi and seem to have a natural affinity for Cajun spices. They are absolutely heavenly that way, but the addition of watercress sauce livens them up even more.

serves 4

1–2 tablespoons Cajun Spice Mix (see Note)

1 1/2 pounds catfish

watercress sauce:

1 bunch watercress, stems removed

1 tablespoon Dijon mustard

3 tablespoons Yogurt Cheese (page 19)

2 tablespoons fresh orange juice

Rub spice mix into both sides of catfish, cover, and refrigerate for 1 hour.

Place watercress in the bowl of a food processor fitted with a steel blade and pulse until the watercress is finely chopped. Add remaining ingredients and puree.

In the meantime, prepare grill or broiler. Cook catfish about 7 minutes on each side, depending on thickness, or until fish flakes easily. Serve with chilled sauce on the side or underneath as a coulis.

NOTE:

To make Cajun Spice Mix, combine the following ingredients:

1 teaspoon dried Greek oregano

1/2 teaspoon cayenne pepper

1/2 teaspoon black pepper

1 teaspoon garlic powder

1 teaspoon dried thyme

1/2 teaspoon Hungarian paprika

1/2 teaspoon salt

per serving

Calories	180	Cholesterol	99.8 mg
Protein	29.5 g	Calcium	74.8 mg
Carbohydrates	2.16 g	Iron	.632 mg
Fat—Total	5.34 g	Sodium	135 mg

dry rubbed swordfish steaks

Although swordfish is available all year round, it's at its best in the summer.

serves 4

$^{1}/_{2}$ teaspoon onion powder

$^{1}/_{2}$ teaspoon garlic powder

$^{1}/_{2}$ teaspoon cayenne pepper

$^{1}/_{2}$ teaspoon dried Greek oregano

$^{1}/_{2}$ teaspoon dried thyme

$^{1}/_{2}$ teaspoon dried basil

1 teaspoon salt

1 teaspoon black pepper

1 teaspoon Hungarian paprika

1$^{1}/_{2}$ pounds swordfish

Combine onion powder, garlic powder, cayenne, oregano, thyme, basil, salt, pepper, and paprika in a small bowl. Vigorously rub into both sides of swordfish. Let sit in refrigerator for no more than 2 hours. Prepare broiler or grill.

Place swordfish on grill or under broiler and cook until the flesh is white, about 4 minutes on each side, depending on thickness, or until fish flakes easily.

per serving

Calories	206	Cholesterol	66.3 mg
Protein	33.6 g	Calcium	7.42 mg
Carbohydrates	0 g	Iron	1.38 mg
Fat—Total	6.82 g	Sodium	685 mg

yellow fin tuna with dilled mustard sauce

1 1/2 pounds yellow fin tuna, about 1 1/2–2 inches thick

1 tablespoon chopped fresh dill

2 tablespoons Dijon mustard

1/4 cup fresh lemon juice (about 1 lemon)

1/4 teaspoon black pepper

Place tuna in a shallow glass or ceramic pan. Combine dill, mustard, lemon juice, and black pepper in a small bowl and pour over tuna. Cover and refrigerate for no more than 2 hours.

Prepare grill or broiler. Remove tuna from marinade and place on grill or under broiler. Reserve marinade. Grill about 3 minutes on each side or until fish flakes easily.

While tuna is cooking, place marinade ingredients in a small saucepan and bring to a boil over high heat. Divide tuna into four serving pieces and pour marinade over each.

per serving

Calories	183	Cholesterol	53.6 mg
Protein	34.5 g	Calcium	13 mg
Carbohydrates	1.83 g	Iron	.934 mg
Fat—Total	3.52 g	Sodium	598 mg

tuna with roasted red pepper and basil

1 1/4 pounds tuna

roasted bell pepper sauce:

2 roasted red bell peppers (page 21), coarsely chopped

2 garlic cloves, peeled and finely chopped or pressed

1/2 cup coarsely chopped fresh basil leaves

1/2 cup fresh lemon juice (about 2 lemons)

2 tablespoons balsamic vinegar

Salt and pepper to taste

Arrange tuna in a shallow pan in one layer. Combine peppers, garlic, basil, lemon juice, and balsamic vinegar in a medium-size bowl. Set aside until ready to use.

Prepare grill or broiler. Place tuna on grill or under broiler and cook for about 3 minutes on each side or until fish flakes easily. Salt and pepper to taste.

Cut into four serving pieces and serve with sauce on the side or ladle sauce onto four plates and arrange tuna on each.

per serving

Calories	177	Cholesterol	47.6 mg
Protein	30.9 g	Calcium	21.3 mg
Carbohydrates	6.19 g	Iron	1.1 mg
Fat—Total	2.94 g	Sodium	446 mg

portuguese fish stew

Quick to prepare, nutritious and hearty to eat, and beautiful to look at, Portuguese Fish Stew is perfect fare all year round.

serves 4

3 garlic cloves, peeled and finely chopped

1 teaspoon dried basil

$^1/_4$ teaspoon crushed red pepper flakes

1 cup chopped fresh tomatoes

1 cup bottled clam juice

$^1/_2$ cup dry white wine

$^1/_2$ cup fish or Chicken Stock (page 18) or low-sodium canned or from bouillon cube

6 small red new potatoes, quartered and boiled (pieces should be the size of the scallops)

1 pound filleted assorted chowder fish (such as scrod, cod, halibut, or cusk)

$^1/_4$ pound raw shrimp, shelled and deveined

$^1/_3$ pound raw sea scallops

$^1/_4$ cup chopped fresh parsley

Heat a large nonstick skillet and add garlic. Cook over low heat until golden. If garlic begins to stick, add a small amount of water. Add basil, pepper flakes, and tomatoes and cook 5 minutes. Add clam juice, wine, stock, and potatoes and cook 5 more minutes. Add chowder fish, shrimp, and scallops, cover pan, and simmer another 5 minutes over low heat. Add parsley just before serving.

per serving

Calories	262	Cholesterol	106 mg
Protein	35.4 g	Calcium	71 mg
Carbohydrates	19.7 g	Iron	2.67 mg
Fat—Total	1.99 g	Sodium	403 mg

cilantro shrimp

Fresh cilantro is one of the few herbs for which absolutely, under no circumstances, should the dried variety be substituted. Wait until you can get fresh cilantro before making this dish.

serves 4

$^1/_2$ teaspoon salt

$^1/_2$ teaspoon ground cumin

$^1/_4$ teaspoon cayenne pepper

$^1/_4$ teaspoon black pepper

$^1/_4$ teaspoon dried Greek oregano

1 teaspoon garlic powder

1 teaspoon chili powder

1 teaspoon Hungarian paprika

24 large raw shrimp, peeled and deveined

sauce:

1 cup chopped fresh cilantro leaves

1 garlic clove, peeled and chopped

1 shallot, peeled and sliced

$^1/_3$ cup orange juice

1 tablespoon hot water

1 tablespoon olive oil

Combine salt, cumin, cayenne, pepper, oregano, garlic powder, chili powder, and paprika in a small bowl. Rub mixture over shrimp, cover, and refrigerate at least 2 hours.

In the meantime, make the sauce. Combine cilantro, garlic, and shallot in a food processor fitted with a steel blade. Pulse until garlic is chopped. While the machine is running, slowly add orange juice, hot water, and olive oil. Blend until thoroughly combined. Set aside.

Prepare grill or broiler. Cook shrimp about 2 minutes on each side or until they turn pink. Serve with sauce on top or on the side.

per serving

Calories	89.7	Cholesterol	63.9 mg
Protein	8.95 g	Calcium	31.2 mg
Carbohydrates	3.87 g	Iron	1.23 mg
Fat—Total	4.17 g	Sodium	331 mg

spicy shrimp with garlic and orange glaze

serves 4

1 pound large raw shrimp, shelled and deveined

4 garlic cloves, peeled and finely chopped or pressed

1 teaspoon dried basil

$1/2$ teaspoon crushed red pepper flakes

$1/2$ cup dry white wine

$1/4$ cup orange juice

Heat a large nonstick skillet and add garlic. Cook over low heat about 5 minutes or until golden. Add basil, pepper flakes, wine, and orange juice. Raise heat to high and bring to a boil. Reduce heat to low and simmer for about 5 minutes or until liquid is reduced by half.

Add shrimp to pan and cook over high heat about 2–3 minutes until shrimp turn pink, turning occasionally. Serve immediately.

per serving

Calories	152	Cholesterol	173 mg
Protein	23.3 g	Calcium	68.9 mg
Carbohydrates	3.87 g	Iron	2.91 mg
Fat—Total	2.01 g	Sodium	170 mg

shrimp with orange and fennel

Shrimp and fennel combine perfectly, but don't hesitate to try this recipe with scallops.

serves 4

$^1/_3$ cup fresh orange juice (about 1 orange)

2 teaspoons grated orange peel

2 tablespoons sambuca or Pernod

$^1/_2$ cup finely diced fresh fennel bulb

1 fresh tomato, diced

$^1/_4$ teaspoon black pepper

$^1/_4$ teaspoon salt

1 $^1/_2$ pounds extra-large raw shrimp, peeled and deveined

Fresh orange slices (for garnish)

In a small bowl, combine orange juice, orange peel, sambuca or Pernod, fennel, tomato, pepper, and salt and set aside.

Heat a large cast-iron skillet until it is so hot a drop of water bounces off it. Add shrimp and cook for 2–3 minutes per side or until they turn pink.

Add orange juice mixture and cook about 1 minute or until it is warmed through.

Garnish with orange slices.

per serving

Calories	226	Cholesterol	259 mg
Protein	35.1 g	Calcium	98 mg
Carbohydrates	9.22 g	Iron	4.36 mg
Fat—Total	3.13 g	Sodium	394 mg

shrimp with chipotle barbecue sauce

Chipotle chilies are smoked jalapeño peppers. Although they are not available everywhere, they're worth seeking out. Smoky chipotle chili makes a great sauce for both shrimp and scallops.

serves 4

sauce:

I canned chipotle chili in adobo sauce, unrinsed and finely chopped

3 garlic cloves, peeled and finely chopped

2 scallions, chopped

I tomato, finely diced

I teaspoon dried Greek oregano

$1/4$ teaspoon salt

$1/4$ cup fresh lime juice (about 2 limes)

12 fresh basil leaves, julienned

$1^1/2$ pounds extra-large raw shrimp, peeled and deveined

In a small bowl, combine chipotle chili, garlic, scallions, tomato, oregano, salt, lime juice, and basil leaves and set aside.

Meanwhile, prepare the grill or broiler. Cook shrimp over very high heat for 2–3 minutes per side or until they turn pink.

Cover shrimp with chipotle sauce and serve immediately.

per serving

Calories	197	Cholesterol	259 mg
Protein	35.1 g	Calcium	102 mg
Carbohydrates	5.78 g	Iron	4.42 mg
Fat—Total	3.09 g	Sodium	439 mg

oriental scallion ginger shrimp

Stir fry your way into health.

16 large raw shrimp (about 1–1¼ pounds), cleaned and deveined

1 teaspoon white sugar or sugar substitute

2 tablespoons soy sauce

2 tablespoons dry sherry

1 tablespoon cornstarch

1 teaspoon peanut, safflower, or canola oil

3 bunches scallions, including green, cut into 2-inch pieces

1 quarter-size slice fresh gingerroot, peeled, if desired, and finely chopped

4 carrots, thinly sliced on the diagonal

3 celery stalks, halved lengthwise and thinly sliced on the diagonal

1–2 red bell peppers, cored, seeded, and thinly sliced

2 tablespoons chopped fresh basil

Combine the shrimp, sugar, soy sauce, sherry, and cornstarch in a shallow glass or ceramic bowl and set aside.

Heat a large wok over a high flame and add the oil. Add scallions and ginger and cook for 2–3 minutes.

Add carrots, celery, and bell pepper and cook for about 5 minutes more or until the vegetables have just begun to soften.

Add shrimp mixture and cook, stirring all the while, until the shrimp turns pink. Add basil and serve immediately.

per serving

Calories	237	Cholesterol	216 mg
Protein	31.1 g	Calcium	137 mg
Carbohydrates	17.9 g	Iron	4.8 mg
Fat—Total	3.89 g	Sodium	782 mg

mustard bluefish

Nothing goes better with bluefish than mustard. Two types of mustard make this recipe twice as good.

serves 4

1 large or 4 small bluefish fillets (about 1 ½ pounds)

½ cup grainy Dijon mustard

½ cup smooth Dijon mustard

2 large leeks, cleaned and thinly sliced

1 cup fish stock

1 cup dry white wine

Preheat oven to 350 degrees.

Place bluefish in a baking dish and cover with mustard. Place leeks on top of fish. Pour fish stock and white wine around fish and place in oven. Bake for about 15 minutes or until fish flakes easily. Remove fish to a serving platter and set aside. Pour liquid and leeks into a small saucepan and bring to a low boil over medium heat. Cook for about 5 minutes or until liquid is reduced by about one third. Serve sauce on side or over fish.

per serving

Calories	337	Cholesterol	102 mg
Protein	38.2 g	Calcium	114 mg
Carbohydrates	13.3 g	Iron	3.74 mg
Fat—Total	10.3 g	Sodium	1029 mg

arctic char with sambuca

By adding arctic char to your repertoire of fish dishes, you'll be adding a salmon-like fish—but one lighter in taste, texture, and cost.

serves 4

$^1/_8$ – $^1/_4$ teaspoon garlic powder

1 tablespoon sambuca

1 $^1/_2$ pounds arctic char

Orange slices (for garnish)

Rub garlic powder and sambuca into both sides of arctic char and refrigerate for 2 hours.

Prepare the grill or broiler. Cook for about 4 minutes on each side or until fish flakes easily.

Serve garnished with orange slices.

per serving

Calories	319	Cholesterol	113 mg
Protein	34 g	Calcium	37.5 mg
Carbohydrates	1.66 g	Iron	1.21 mg
Fat—Total	17.7 g	Sodium	80.2 mg

chicken

chinese bbq chicken

A delightful and lively alternative to traditional barbecue, this marinade and technique works equally well with steak or turkey cutlets.

serves 4

4 (6-ounce) boneless and skinless chicken breasts

2 tablespoons hoisin sauce

2 tablespoons tomato ketchup

2 tablespoons Japanese rice wine vinegar

4 garlic cloves, peeled and finely chopped

2 quarter-size slices fresh gingerroot, peeled, if desired, and finely chopped

$^{1}/_{2}$ teaspoon Chinese chili paste or more, to taste

$^{1}/_{2}$ cup Chicken Stock (page 18) or low-sodium canned or from bouillon cube

Place chicken in a large shallow glass or ceramic bowl and add remaining ingredients, except chicken stock. Cover and refrigerate 4 hours or overnight.

Remove chicken from bowl and reserve marinade.

Heat a large nonstick or cast-iron skillet over high heat. When the skillet is hot, add the chicken, reduce the heat to medium, and cook until the juices run clear, about 5–10 minutes per side, depending on thickness of chicken. This may have to be done in two batches. Remove chicken from the pan and add chicken stock and reserved marinade. Bring to a boil over high heat and pour over chicken or serve as a sauce on the side.

per serving

Calories	204	Cholesterol	98.6 mg
Protein	40.3 g	Calcium	27.3 mg
Carbohydrates	3.65 g	Iron	1.44 mg
Fat—Total	2.33 g	Sodium	211 mg

oriental curried chicken

4 (6-ounce) boneless and skinless chicken breasts

2 tablespoons soy sauce

2 tablespoons Japanese rice vinegar

2 teaspoons curry powder

$^{1}/_{2}$ cup Chicken Stock (page 18) or low-sodium canned or from bouillon cube

Place chicken in a large shallow glass or ceramic bowl and add remaining ingredients, except chicken stock. Cover and refrigerate for 4 hours or overnight.

Prepare grill or broiler. Remove chicken from bowl and reserve marinade. Cook for about 10 minutes on each side, depending on thickness of chicken.

Place reserved marinade in a small saucepan, add chicken stock, and bring to a boil over high heat. Pour over chicken or serve as a sauce on the side.

per serving

Calories	197	Cholesterol	98.6 mg
Protein	40.4 g	Calcium	21.9 mg
Carbohydrates	1.33 g	Iron	1.52 mg
Fat—Total	2.29 g	Sodium	633 mg

honey-glazed chicken breasts with thyme

These chicken breasts are slightly sweet and completely delicious. To show off the flavor, try serving them with a nutty brown rice and a bitter green, such as broccoli rabe.

serves 4

4 (6-ounce) boneless and skinless chicken breasts

1 1/2 tablespoons dried thyme

1/4 cup balsamic vinegar

1/4 cup red wine vinegar

1/4 cup honey

1 celery stalk, halved lengthwise and thinly sliced

2 carrots, quartered lengthwise and thinly sliced

1 small red onion, peeled and chopped

1/2 cup Chicken Stock (page 18) or low-sodium canned or from bouillon cube

Combine all ingredients except for the chicken stock in a large shallow glass or ceramic bowl. Cover and place in the refrigerator for 4 hours.

Remove as much of the marinade as possible from the chicken breasts and set the marinade aside. Heat a nonstick frying pan over medium-high heat and sear the chicken breasts for approximately 3 minutes per side. Remove the chicken breasts from the pan and set aside.

Place the marinade in the pan and add the chicken stock. Bring to a boil over high heat. Reduce heat to low and simmer for 10 minutes. Add chicken and cook until tender, turning often, about 10 more minutes.

per serving

Calories	286	Cholesterol	98.6 mg
Protein	40.8 g	Calcium	43.6 mg
Carbohydrates	25.3 g	Iron	1.88 mg
Fat—Total	2.44 g	Sodium	143 mg

grilled chicken with parsley sauce

Wonderful on chicken, this lush, green sauce also makes a great topping for pasta.

serves 4

sauce:

1/2 cup finely chopped fresh parsley

2 tablespoons Chicken Stock (page 18) or low-sodium canned or from bouillon cube

1/2 cup fresh lemon juice (about 2 lemons)

2 teaspoons Dijon mustard

1/4 teaspoon salt

Pepper to taste

4 (6-ounce) boneless and skinless chicken breasts

Place all sauce ingredients in the bowl of a food processor fitted with a steel blade. Process until smooth.

Prepare the grill or broiler. Cook chicken until the juices run clear, about 10 minutes on each side, depending on thickness. Place cold sauce on chicken and serve immediately.

per serving

Calories	197	Cholesterol	98.6 mg
Protein	39.7 g	Calcium	23.5 mg
Carbohydrates	2.83 g	Iron	1.3 mg
Fat—Total	2.31 g	Sodium	279 mg

chicken breasts with basil and chipotle sauce

Spicy and just a tad sweet, this dish is perfect served with steamed white rice and a big green salad.

serves 4

1 canned chipotle chili in adobo sauce, unrinsed

¼ cup chopped fresh basil leaves

2 garlic cloves, peeled

¼ cup Chicken Stock (page 18) or low-sodium canned or from bouillon cube

1 small fresh tomato, diced

4 (6-ounce) boneless and skinless chicken breasts

Place the chipotle chili, basil leaves, and garlic cloves in the bowl of a food processor fitted with a steel blade. Process until smooth. Add chicken stock and tomato and pulse, letting some texture remain. Set aside.

Heat a large nonstick or cast-iron skillet over high heat. When the skillet is hot, add the chicken, reduce the heat to medium, and cook until the juices run clear, about 5–10 minutes per side, depending on thickness of chicken.

This may have to be done in two batches.

Place sauce on chicken and serve immediately.

per serving

Calories	194	Cholesterol	98.6 mg
Protein	39.9 g	Calcium	20.8 mg
Carbohydrates	1.39 g	Iron	1.38 mg
Fat—Total	2.28 g	Sodium	167 mg

chicken breasts with peach and tomato chutney

Although this recipe was created for chicken, it works just as well on pork or steak.

serves 4

2 tablespoons chili powder

1 tablespoon ground cumin

1 teaspoon salt

1 teaspoon white sugar or sugar substitute

$^1/_2$ teaspoon black pepper

4 (6-ounce) boneless and skinless chicken breasts

1 fresh peach, peeled, if desired, and diced

1 fresh tomato, diced

1 red or Spanish onion, peeled and chopped

1 tablespoon chopped fresh cilantro (see headnote, page 74)

Combine chili powder, cumin, salt, sugar, and black pepper in a small bowl. Rub mixture into chicken and refrigerate for 1 hour.

Combine peach, tomato, onion, and cilantro in a medium-size glass or ceramic bowl. Set aside.

Prepare grill or broiler. Cook chicken until the juices run clear, about 10 minutes on each side, depending on thickness. Serve chicken with chutney on the side.

per serving

Calories	228	Cholesterol	98.6 mg
Protein	40.6 g	Calcium	38.2 mg
Carbohydrates	9.31 g	Iron	1.99 mg
Fat—Total	2.9 g	Sodium	685 mg

chicken tandoori

Indians call their grilled chicken tandoori, after the tandoor, the oven in which it is cooked. Even without a tandoor, you can approximate the taste with this method.

4 (6-ounce) boneless and skinless chicken breasts

1 cup nonfat plain yogurt

2 teaspoons curry powder

$^1/_2$ teaspoon ground cardamom

$^1/_4$ teaspoon salt

1 heaping teaspoon Hungarian paprika

$^1/_4$ teaspoon garlic powder

$^1/_4$ teaspoon cayenne pepper

Combine all ingredients in a large shallow glass or ceramic bowl. Cover and refrigerate 4 hours or overnight.

Remove as much of the marinade as possible from the chicken breasts and place in a small saucepan. Bring to a boil over high heat and set aside.

Heat a large nonstick or cast-iron skillet over high heat. When the skillet is hot, add the chicken, reduce the heat to medium, and cook until the juices run clear, about 5–10 minutes per side, depending on thickness of chicken. This may have to be done in two batches.

Serve with marinade over chicken.

per serving

Calories	223	Cholesterol	99.7 mg
Protein	43 g	Calcium	146 mg
Carbohydrates	5.31 g	Iron	1.59 mg
Fat—Total	2.36 g	Sodium	291 mg

chicken breasts with cilantro and sesame

The very small amount of oriental sesame oil in this recipe imparts a large amount of flavor. Don't omit it. It's worth it.

serves 4

4 (6-ounce) boneless and skinless chicken breasts

1 quarter-size slice fresh gingerroot, peeled, if desired, and finely chopped

2 garlic cloves, peeled and finely chopped

$^1/_2$ teaspoon salt

Pinch black pepper

1 teaspoon oriental sesame oil

$^1/_4$ cup fresh lime juice (about 2 limes)

2 tablespoons fresh orange juice

2 tablespoons chopped fresh cilantro (see headnote, page 74)

1 tablespoon toasted sesame seeds

Place chicken in a large shallow glass or ceramic bowl and add remaining ingredients, except cilantro and sesame seeds. Cover and refrigerate 4 hours or overnight.

Remove chicken from bowl and discard marinade.

Heat a large nonstick or cast-iron skillet over high heat. When the skillet is hot, add the chicken, reduce the heat to medium, and cook until the juices run clear, about 5–10 minutes per side, depending on thickness of chicken. This may have to be done in two batches.

To serve, sprinkle cilantro and sesame seeds over cooked chicken.

per serving

Calories	219	Cholesterol	98.6 mg
Protein	40 g	Calcium	45.9 mg
Carbohydrates	3.22 g	Iron	1.6 mg
Fat—Total	4.4 g	Sodium	378 mg

lemon tarragon chicken breasts

4 (6-ounce) boneless and skinless chicken breasts

2 tablespoons dry white wine

3 tablespoons fresh lemon juice

1 tablespoon dried tarragon

2 tablespoons Dijon mustard

1/4 teaspoon black pepper

1/2 teaspoon salt

Place chicken in a large shallow glass or ceramic bowl and add remaining ingredients. Cover and refrigerate 4 hours.

Preheat the oven to 350 degrees.

Remove chicken from bowl and discard marinade. Place chicken in a heavy casserole or baking dish and bake until the juices run clear, about 20–25 minutes, depending on thickness of chicken.

per serving

Calories	200	Cholesterol	98.6 mg
Protein	39.8 g	Calcium	27.1 mg
Carbohydrates	1.55 g	Iron	1.41 mg
Fat—Total	2.48 g	Sodium	475 mg

lemon and sage chicken breasts

4 (6-ounce) boneless and skinless chicken breasts

3 ¼ cups Chicken Stock (page 18) or low-sodium canned or from bouillon cubes

2 carrots, sliced

I large or 2 small shallots, peeled and sliced

8 fresh sage leaves

I teaspoon dried sage

2 garlic cloves, peeled and chopped

Zest of I lemon

Heat a nonstick skillet over medium-high heat. Place chicken breasts in skillet and cook until just browned on both sides. Remove chicken breasts and set aside. Do not wash the pan.

To the same pan, add ¼ cup chicken stock. Add carrots, shallots, sage leaves, dried sage, and garlic cloves and cook over medium heat, until the shallots are golden, about 10 minutes.

Add lemon zest and the remaining chicken stock and bring to a boil. Reduce heat to low and simmer 10 minutes. Add the reserved chicken and simmer 10 more minutes.

per serving

Calories	242	Cholesterol	98.6 mg
Protein	44 g	Calcium	42.7 mg
Carbohydrates	6.59 g	Iron	1.96 mg
Fat—Total	3.36 g	Sodium	183 mg

souvlaki chicken breasts

Souvlaki chicken can be made with whole chicken breasts, as described below, or with chunks of chicken, skewered on sticks. If you use chunks, alternate chicken with peppers and tomatoes, and bake 12–15 minutes.

serves 4

4 (6-ounce) boneless and skinless chicken breasts

1 shallot, peeled and thinly sliced

1 tablespoon chopped fresh oregano

1/4 cup fresh lemon juice (about 1 lemon)

1/4 teaspoon salt

1/4 teaspoon black pepper

1 red bell pepper, seeded and sliced or diced

1 yellow bell pepper, seeded and sliced or diced

1 cup cherry tomatoes

Place chicken in a large shallow glass or ceramic bowl and add remaining ingredients, except peppers and tomatoes. Cover and refrigerate 4 hours.

Preheat oven to 350 degrees.

Remove chicken from bowl and discard marinade. Place chicken in a heavy casserole or baking dish with the peppers and tomatoes and bake until juices run clear, about 20–25 minutes, depending on thickness of chicken.

per serving

Calories	218	Cholesterol	98.6 mg
Protein	40.5 g	Calcium	30.3 mg
Carbohydrates	7.88 g	Iron	1.74 mg
Fat—Total	2.38 g	Sodium	249 mg

chicken breasts with red onions and oranges

Your guests will never guess the spices that combine to make this tasty chicken, and, because it's so delicious, they won't care!

serves 4

4 (6-ounce) boneless and skinless chicken breasts

Juice of 2 limes

2 garlic cloves, peeled and finely chopped

$1/4$ teaspoon salt

$1/4$ teaspoon cayenne pepper

1 teaspoon ground cinnamon

1 teaspoon chili powder

$1/4$ teaspoon ground cumin

1 red onion, peeled and thinly sliced

1 orange, thinly sliced

Place chicken in a large shallow glass or ceramic bowl and add remaining ingredients, except onion and orange. Cover and refrigerate 4 hours or overnight.

Prepare grill or broiler. Remove chicken from bowl and place on a rack with the onion and orange. Cook until the juices run clear, about 10 minutes on each side, depending on thickness of chicken.

per serving

Calories	216	Cholesterol	98.6 mg
Protein	40.1 g	Calcium	40.7 mg
Carbohydrates	7.72 g	Iron	1.37 mg
Fat—Total	2.24 g	Sodium	245 mg

peppery chicken breasts

The fresh watercress in peppery chicken breasts adds an interesting tang to this slightly spicy chicken dish. Serve with Garlic Mashed Potatoes (page 175) and lots of fresh, ripe tomatoes (as a side dish).

serves 4

4 (6-ounce) boneless and skinless chicken breasts

4 garlic cloves, peeled and chopped

1 tablespoon dried Greek oregano

1 teaspoon dried thyme

1 teaspoon crushed red pepper flakes

$^{1}/_{4}$ cup balsamic vinegar

1 (28-ounce) can whole peeled tomatoes, including liquid

$^{1}/_{2}$ cup coarsely chopped fresh basil

$^{1}/_{2}$ bunch fresh watercress

Freshly grated Parmesan cheese

Place chicken in a large shallow glass or ceramic bowl and add garlic, oregano, thyme, red pepper flakes, and balsamic vinegar. Cover and refrigerate at least 4 hours or overnight.

Heat a large cast-iron or nonstick skillet over medium heat. Add the chicken breasts and brown on both sides.

Add the tomatoes and their juice and reduce the heat to low. Cook until the chicken is tender, about 20–25 minutes. Add the basil and watercress and cook until wilted, about 5 minutes more.

Serve with freshly grated Parmesan cheese.

per serving

Calories	304	Cholesterol	98.6 mg
Protein	48.2 g	Calcium	487 mg
Carbohydrates	22 g	Iron	11 mg
Fat—Total	4.2 g	Sodium	446 mg

chicken breasts marbella

4 (6-ounce) boneless and skinless chicken breasts

2 garlic cloves, peeled and chopped

2 tablespoons dried Greek oregano

$^1/_4$ cup dry white wine

2 tablespoons red wine vinegar

8 prunes, pitted

8 dried apricots

3 tablespoons brown sugar or brown sugar substitute

$^1/_4$ teaspoon salt

2 bay leaves

Place chicken in a large shallow glass or ceramic baking dish and add remaining ingredients. Cover and refrigerate for 4 hours or overnight.

Preheat oven to 350 degrees.

Place entire contents of the baking dish, including marinade, in the oven and bake for about 20 minutes or until chicken is tender. Remove bay leaves before serving.

per serving

Calories	281	Cholesterol	98.6 mg
Protein	40.2 g	Calcium	40.9 mg
Carbohydrates	22.5 g	Iron	2.22 mg
Fat—Total	2.23 g	Sodium	249 mg

quickest herb and spice chicken

When you have no time to cook and want to eat well, this quick chicken dish will satisfy every time.

serves 4

4 (6-ounce) boneless and skinless chicken breasts

1 teaspoon salt

1 teaspoon black pepper

$^1/_2$ teaspoon cayenne pepper (optional)

$^1/_2$ teaspoon dried thyme

1 teaspoon dried basil

$^1/_2$ teaspoon dried Greek oregano

1 teaspoon onion powder

Place chicken in a large shallow glass or ceramic bowl. Combine all the spices and rub into chicken.

Heat a large cast-iron or nonstick skillet over medium heat and add the chicken breasts. Cook until the juices run clear, about 7 minutes on each side, depending on thickness of chicken.

per serving

Calories	190	Cholesterol	98.6 mg
Protein	39.5 g	Calcium	31.6 mg
Carbohydrates	1.01 g	Iron	1.55 mg
Fat—Total	2.14 g	Sodium	644 mg

ricotta and herb stuffed chicken breasts

Perfect for a summer picnic, ricotta and herb stuffed chicken breasts are even better cold than hot. Serve with Tuscan Bread Salad (page 204) and pears and you have an ideal meal for a special afternoon.

serves 4

4 (6-ounce) boneless and skinless chicken breasts

10 tablespoons nonfat or part-skim ricotta cheese

1 tablespoon finely chopped fresh parsley

1 tablespoon finely chopped fresh basil

$1/2$ teaspoon dried tarragon

$1/2$ teaspoon dried thyme

$1/2$ teaspoon dried marjoram

$1/4 - 1/2$ teaspoon black pepper

4 slices of tomato

Preheat oven to 350 degrees.

Pound breasts until thin as possible; trim away excess fat.

Mix remaining ingredients, except for the tomato, and place a quarter of the mixture in the center of each breast. Fold the edges of the breasts in over the filling so that the chicken completely envelops the cheese.

Top with tomato slices, place in a baking pan, and bake in the oven for 15 minutes.

Raise heat to broil and cook 5 minutes more or until tomato is browned.

per serving

Calories	242	Cholesterol	110 mg
Protein	43.9 g	Calcium	124 mg
Carbohydrates	2.68 g	Iron	1.46 mg
Fat—Total	5.2 g	Sodium	160 mg

whole roasted five-spice chicken

A touch of the Orient comes to roast chicken with this lightly spiced recipe.

serves 4 with leftovers

1 (6-pound) roaster chicken, giblets and neck removed, chicken washed well with several changes of cold water

$^1/_4$ cup light soy sauce

2 tablespoons dry sherry

1 tablespoon brown sugar or brown sugar substitute

2–3 teaspoons five-spice powder

3 quarter-size slices of fresh gingerroot, peeled, if desired, and finely chopped

3 garlic cloves, peeled and finely chopped

Place chicken in a large bowl or pan and add remaining ingredients. Rub vigorously into chicken. Cover and refrigerate overnight.

Preheat oven to 500 degrees.

Place chicken on a rack in a roasting pan and cook for about 1 hour or until the juices run clear at the thigh joint.

After cooking, remove skin for lower calories and fat.

per serving

Calories	230	Cholesterol	94.8 mg
Protein	31 g	Calcium	18.5 mg
Carbohydrates	3.57 g	Iron	1.51 mg
Fat—Total	8.45 g	Sodium	603 mg

whole roast chicken with vegetable paste

This guaranteed-to-be-moist whole roast chicken will be a family favorite.

serves 4 with leftovers

1 teaspoon dried tarragon

1 teaspoon dried thyme

1 teaspoon dried rosemary

$^1/_2$ teaspoon kosher salt

1 tablespoon black pepper

10–12 garlic cloves, peeled and finely chopped

1 tablespoon balsamic vinegar

1 (6-pound) roaster chicken, giblets and neck removed, chicken washed well with several changes of cold water

2 stalks celery, diced

2 carrots, diced

1 red onion, peeled and diced

Combine tarragon, thyme, rosemary, salt, pepper, garlic, and balsamic vinegar and blend, by hand, until paste-like. Rub chicken vigorously inside and out with the paste. Cover and refrigerate at least 2 hours.

Preheat oven to 500 degrees.

Combine celery, carrots, and onion and place in chicken cavity.

Place chicken on a rack in a roasting pan and cook for about 1 hour or until the juices run clear at the thigh joint.

Remove skin for lower calories and fat.

per serving

Calories	212	Cholesterol	90.7 mg
Protein	30.4 g	Calcium	39 mg
Carbohydrates	6.6 g	Iron	1.58 mg
Fat—Total	6.64 g	Sodium	382 mg

whole rosemary chicken

Fresh rosemary perfumes chicken in a unique and wonderful way.

6 garlic cloves, peeled and finely chopped

3 sprigs fresh rosemary

1 teaspoon finely chopped fresh lemon peel

$1/2$ teaspoon kosher salt

$1/2$ teaspoon black pepper

Juice of 1 lemon

1 (4–5 pound) roaster chicken, giblets and neck removed, chicken washed well with several changes of cold water

Combine garlic cloves, rosemary, lemon peel, salt, pepper, and lemon juice and blend, by hand, until paste-like. Rub chicken inside and out with the paste. Cover and refrigerate at least 2 hours.

Preheat oven to 500 degrees.

Place chicken on a rack in a roasting pan and cook for about 1 hour or until the juices run clear at the thigh joint.

Remove skin for lower calories and fat.

per serving

Calories	187	Cholesterol	90.7 mg
Protein	29.6 g	Calcium	15.3 mg
Carbohydrates	1.32 g	Iron	1.2 mg
Fat—Total	6.49 g	Sodium	352 mg

whole roast chicken with butternut squash and pears

This is a dangerous dish to make. Don't be surprised when there's nothing left at the end.

serves 4

1 teaspoon dried rosemary

1 teaspoon dried thyme

1 teaspoon dried sage

$^1/_2$ teaspoon kosher salt

$^1/_2$ teaspoon black pepper

1 (6-pound) roaster chicken, giblets and neck removed, chicken washed well with several changes of cold water

$^1/_2$ large butternut squash, seeded, peeled, and cubed

2 Bosc pears, peeled if desired, and cubed

1 small red onion, peeled and quartered

6 garlic cloves, peeled

Preheat oven to 450 degrees.

Combine herbs, salt, and pepper and vigorously rub inside and outside of chicken.

Place on a rack in a large roasting pan and surround with squash, pears, onion, and garlic. Roast for 60–70 minutes or until the juices run clear at the thigh joint.

Remove skin for lower calories and fat.

per serving

Calories	285	Cholesterol	90.7 mg
Protein	31.3 g	Calcium	81.3 mg
Carbohydrates	26 g	Iron	2.24 mg
Fat—Total	6.94 g	Sodium	357 mg

herbed chicken thighs with lemon zest and mint

8 chicken thighs, skinless

1 teaspoon kosher salt

$^{1}/_{2}$ teaspoon black pepper

Juice of 1 lemon

$^{1}/_{2}$ Spanish onion, peeled and chopped

2 garlic cloves, peeled and finely chopped

$^{1}/_{2}$ cup coarsely chopped basil leaves

1 tablespoon finely chopped fresh rosemary

1 teaspoon dried sage

1 tablespoon finely chopped fresh mint

1 heaping teaspoon finely chopped lemon zest

$^{1}/_{4}$ cup finely chopped fresh parsley

Place chicken in a large shallow glass or ceramic bowl or pan. Combine remaining ingredients and rub into chicken. Cover and refrigerate overnight.

Preheat oven to 400 degrees.

Place chicken thighs on a baking sheet, in a single layer. Bake for about 20 minutes, turning occasionally.

per serving

Calories	228	Cholesterol	98.8 mg
Protein	27.5 g	Calcium	30.3 mg
Carbohydrates	2.97 g	Iron	1.8 mg
Fat—Total	11.4 g	Sodium	627 mg

thai chicken breasts with cilantro and mint

This dish is definitely an entree that can stand on its own, but it's also like a very hearty soup: a flavorful broth that's easy to make, chock-full of chicken, vegetables, and fresh herbs.

serves 8

$2^{1}/_{2}$–3 pounds boneless and skinless chicken breasts

8 cups Chicken Stock (page 18) or low-sodium canned or from bouillon cubes

Zest of $^{1}/_{4}$ lime and juice of 1 lime

3 quarter-size slices of fresh gingerroot, unpeeled

1 bay leaf

1 garlic clove, peeled

5 sprigs plus $^{1}/_{3}$ cup chopped fresh cilantro (see headnote, page 74)

5 sprigs plus $^{1}/_{3}$ cup chopped fresh mint

$^{1}/_{4}$ teaspoon crushed red pepper flakes

2 leeks

4 carrots, julienned

2 celery stalks, peeled and julienned

$^{1}/_{4}$ pound dry capellini or other thin spaghetti

$^{1}/_{3}$ cup chopped fresh basil

Place chicken, chicken stock, lime zest, gingerroot, bay leaf, garlic, 5 sprigs cilantro, 5 sprigs mint, and pepper flakes in a 6- or 8-quart stockpot and bring to a low boil over medium heat. Reduce heat to low and cook for about 7 minutes or until the chicken is thoroughly cooked. Remove chicken and place it in the refrigerator. Return stockpot to stove and cook over low heat for an additional 30 minutes. When the chicken is cool enough to handle, shred it.

Quarter leeks lengthwise and wash by soaking them in several changes of water, being careful to get rid of all the sand. Julienne the leeks.

Strain soup through a strainer or colander into a bowl. Discard all but the broth.

Return broth to stockpot, bring to a boil over high heat, add leeks, carrots, and celery, and cook for about 10 minutes or until the carrots are tender. Add capellini and cook for about 5 minutes.

Just prior to serving, add reserved shredded chicken and cilantro, mint, and basil. Cook just until chicken is heated through.

per serving

Calories	281	Cholesterol	90.4 mg
Protein	43.2 g	Calcium	46 mg
Carbohydrates	16.4 g	Iron	2.61 mg
Fat—Total	3.69 g	Sodium	188 mg

turkey chili

Yes, there is such a thing as healthy chili and turkey makes the difference.

serves 8

$^1/_2$ cup water

2 Spanish onions, peeled and coarsely chopped

4 cloves garlic, peeled and finely chopped

I red bell pepper, seeded and coarsely chopped

I green bell pepper, seeded and coarsely chopped

I tablespoon dried Greek oregano

2 teaspoons dried basil

2 teaspoons chili powder

2 teaspoons crushed red pepper flakes

I tablespoon ground cumin or more, to taste

I teaspoon cayenne pepper (optional)

2 cups cooked white beans (about I $^1/_4$ cups dried; see Note, page 35)

2 cups cooked black beans

4 (I-pound) cans dark red kidney beans, drained and rinsed

2 (20-ounce) cans whole tomatoes, coarsely chopped, including liquid

I pound boneless and skinless turkey breast

Chopped fresh cilantro (see headnote, page 74) or basil

Place water, onions, garlic, peppers, and spices in a 6- or 8-quart stockpot and cook over low heat, covered, until vegetables begin to wilt, about 15 minutes.

Add beans and tomatoes and cook, covered, for 1 hour, stirring occasionally.

While the chili is cooking, poach the turkey breast. Place turkey breast in a single layer in a large skillet. Cover with water and bring to a low boil over medium heat. Reduce heat to low and simmer for about 7 minutes or until turkey is fully cooked. Set aside until cool enough to handle. Shred and add to chili with fresh basil or cilantro just prior to serving.

per serving

Calories	441	Cholesterol	35.3 mg
Protein	37.7 g	Calcium	158 mg
Carbohydrates	70.6 g	Iron	9.81 mg
Fat—Total	2.25 g	Sodium	268 mg

spicy grilled chicken thighs

Meaty and satisfying chicken thighs are a tasty and exotic change from chicken breasts. These can be served hot or cold.

serves 4

1 tablespoon curry powder

1 tablespoon ground cumin

1 tablespoon paprika

2 teaspoons ground ginger

2 teaspoons kosher salt

2 teaspoons white pepper

8 chicken thighs, skinless

Combine spices in a small bowl and rub into chicken. Place chicken in a medium-size shallow bowl, cover and refrigerate overnight.

Preheat broiler.

Place chicken thighs on broiler pan 6 inches from heat and cook about 10 minutes on each side or until golden brown.

per serving

Calories	229	Cholesterol	98.8 mg
Protein	27.5 g	Calcium	25.3 mg
Carbohydrates	2.51 g	Iron	2.34 mg
Fat—Total	11.8 g	Sodium	1159 mg

beef, pork, and veal

classic beef stew

1 pound beef stew meat, trimmed of all fat, cut into 1-inch cubes

1 Spanish onion, peeled and chopped

3 garlic cloves, peeled and finely chopped

1 pound carrots, diced

1 tablespoon dried thyme

2–3 celery stalks, diced

2 tablespoons all-purpose white flour

2 cups beef stock

1 cup red wine

8 sun-dried tomatoes, chopped

2 large or 4 small potatoes, cubed

Heat a large cast-iron or nonstick skillet over medium heat, about 5 minutes or until a drop of water flicked into it bursts into droplets. Add the beef cubes, a few at a time, and brown on all sides. Set aside. This will take several batches. Do not wash the pan.

When all the beef has been browned, add onions, garlic, carrots, thyme, and celery to the same pan and cook, over medium heat, about 10 minutes or until the vegetables begin to brown.

Gradually stir in flour. When the flour has all browned and been fully incorporated, slowly add beef stock and wine, stirring all the time. Add the sun-dried tomatoes and reduce the heat to low. Continue simmering for about 2 more hours or until the meat is tender and the vegetables have softened.

In a separate pot, boil the potatoes for about 10–15 minutes or until tender. Add potatoes to the stew just prior to serving.

per serving

Calories	492	Cholesterol	71.7 mg
Protein	29.2 g	Calcium	76.6 mg
Carbohydrates	46.9 g	Iron	5.21 mg
Fat—Total	16.8 g	Sodium	244 mg

meatballs and spaghetti

An old standby, minus the fat.

tomato sauce:

$1/4$ cup water or Vegetable or Chicken Stock (page 17 or page 18) or low-sodium canned or from bouillon cube

$1/2$ Spanish onion, peeled and finely chopped

3 garlic cloves, peeled and finely chopped or crushed

2 tablespoons dried basil

1 tablespoon dried Greek oregano

$1/2$ teaspoon crushed red pepper flakes

2 (28-ounce) cans whole tomatoes, including liquid

2 tablespoons tomato paste

$1/2$ cup red wine

Pinch sugar

meatballs:

$1 1/3$ pounds ground turkey (93 percent fat-free)

3 scallions, including greens, coarsely chopped

1 teaspoon dried basil

1 teaspoon dried Greek oregano

$1/2$ teaspoon black pepper

$1/2$ cup finely chopped fresh parsley

$1/2$ cup nonfat ricotta cheese

1 pound spaghetti

To make the tomato sauce, place water (or stock), onion, and garlic in a heavy-bottomed 6- or 8-quart stockpot and cook, over medium-low heat, for about 10 minutes or until onion is translucent.

Increase heat to medium, add remaining sauce ingredients, and cook, partially covered, 1½–2 hours, depending upon thickness desired. Stir occasionally.

To make the meatballs, place all the meatball ingredients in a medium-size bowl and combine well. Divide into twenty-four parts and form into balls.

In a nonstick skillet, cook meatballs over medium-high heat until browned on all sides. Cover with tomato sauce and simmer over low heat until cooked through, about 15 minutes.

Bring a large pot of salted water to a boil. Cook the pasta until *al dente*. Serve with meatballs and tomato sauce.

per serving

Calories	567	Cholesterol	81.9 mg
Protein	37.2 g	Calcium	188 mg
Carbohydrates	73 g	Iron	6.77 mg
Fat—Total	12.6 g	Sodium	604 mg

mix-ins for burgers

Burger is king, no matter the meat (veal, beef, or turkey). However, if you're using turkey, add 1 tablespoon cottage cheese or ricotta cheese to make it lighter.

Just mix in any one of the following and you have a great meal. Per 4-ounce burger, add:

1. 1 tablespoon chopped fresh basil and 1 teaspoon Dijon mustard

2. 1 tablespoon chopped fresh basil and 1 tablespoon chopped fresh cilantro (see headnote, page 74)

3. 1 tablespoon bottled barbecue sauce

4. 2 teaspoons light soy sauce and 2 tablespoons chopped water chestnuts

5. 1 tablespoon tomato ketchup, 2 tablespoons chopped onions, and 1 teaspoon minced sun-dried tomatoes

mix-in *only*, for one 4-ounce burger

burger mix-in #1 (basil and mustard)

Calories	4.62	Cholesterol	0 mg
Protein	.312 g	Calcium	8.45 mg
Carbohydrates	.449 g	Iron	.188 mg
Fat—Total	.256 g	Sodium	65.3 mg

for one 4-ounce burger

burger mix-in #2 (basil and cilantro)

Calories	.915	Cholesterol	0 mg
Protein	.091 g	Calcium	5.06 mg
Carbohydrates	.142 g	Iron	.103 mg
Fat—Total	.022 g	Sodium	.386 mg

for one 4-ounce burger

burger mix-in #3 (barbecue sauce)

Calories	11.7	Cholesterol	0 mg
Protein	.281 g	Calcium	2.97 mg
Carbohydrates	2 g	Iron	.141 mg
Fat—Total	.281 g	Sodium	127 mg

for one 4-ounce burger

burger mix-in #4 (soy sauce and water chestnuts)

Calories	26	Cholesterol	0 mg
Protein	1.15 g	Calcium	4.77 mg
Carbohydrates	5.23 g	Iron	.373 mg
Fat—Total	.029 g	Sodium	1029 mg

for one 4-ounce burger

burger mix-in #5 (ketchup, onions, and sun-dried tomatoes)

Calories	26.4	Cholesterol	0 mg
Protein	.624 g	Calcium	8.15 mg
Carbohydrates	6.53 g	Iron	.254 mg
Fat—Total	.121 g	Sodium	206 mg

lemon steak

Tart and peppery, lemon steak is perfect hot or cold.

1 1/2 pounds flank or skirt steak, trimmed of fat

1/2 cup fresh lemon juice (about 2 lemons)

1 teaspoon coarsely ground black pepper

1 red onion, peeled and thinly sliced

Score the steak on both sides with a very sharp knife.

Combine the lemon juice, black pepper, and red onion and pour over the steak in a shallow glass or ceramic container. Cover and refrigerate for 4 hours, turning occasionally.

Remove steak from refrigerator 1 hour before cooking. Prepare grill or broiler. Remove steak from marinade (discard marinade) and place on a rack with the onion. Cook steak for about 3–5 minutes on each side, for rare to medium rare.

Slice the steak across the grain on a diagonal.

per serving

Calories	279	Cholesterol	85.9 mg
Protein	35 g	Calcium	17.9 mg
Carbohydrates	4.65 g	Iron	3.37 mg
Fat—Total	13 g	Sodium	107 mg

diet workshop's recipes for healthy living

spice-rubbed flank steak

Adding wonderful spices to flank steak makes this cut of meat rich, flavorful, and exciting. Spice-rubbed flank steak is great hot, at room temperature, or cold.

serves 4

1 1/4 pounds flank or skirt steak, trimmed of fat

1 teaspoon ground cardamom

1/2 teaspoon kosher salt

2 teaspoons curry powder

1 teaspoon ground cumin

1/2 teaspoon cayenne pepper

1 teaspoon black pepper

1 tablespoon brown sugar or brown sugar substitute

Score the steak on both sides with a very sharp knife.

Combine the remaining ingredients and rub into both sides of steak. Place in a shallow container. Cover and refrigerate at least 4 hours or overnight.

Remove steak from refrigerator 1 hour before cooking. Prepare grill or broiler. Remove steak from marinade (discard marinade) and place on a rack. Cook steak for about 3–5 minutes on each side, for rare to medium rare.

Slice the steak across the grain on a diagonal.

per serving

Calories	249	Cholesterol	76.3 mg
Protein	31 g	Calcium	21.7 mg
Carbohydrates	3.36 g	Iron	3.65 mg
Fat—Total	11.8 g	Sodium	363 mg

balsamic steak

1/2 cup balsamic vinegar

1/2 teaspoon kosher salt

1 teaspoon black pepper

1 1/4 pounds flank or skirt steak, trimmed of fat

Score the steak on both sides with a very sharp knife.

Combine the balsamic vinegar, salt, and black pepper and pour over the steak in a shallow glass or ceramic container. Cover and refrigerate at least 4 hours or overnight, turning occasionally.

Remove steak from refrigerator 1 hour before cooking. Prepare grill or broiler. Remove steak from marinade; discard marinade. Cook steak for about 3–5 minutes on each side, for rare to medium rare.

Slice the steak across the grain on a diagonal.

per serving

Calories	238	Cholesterol	76.3 mg
Protein	30.7 g	Calcium	9.72 mg
Carbohydrates	1.78 g	Iron	3.08 mg
Fat—Total	11.5 g	Sodium	94.8 mg

southwestern steak

This dry rub cooks up well on swordfish and chicken, too.

1 1/2 pounds flank or skirt steak, trimmed of fat

2 teaspoons chili powder

2 teaspoons Hungarian paprika

2 teaspoons garlic powder

2 teaspoons kosher salt

1 1/3 teaspoons cumin

2/3 teaspoon cayenne pepper

2/3 teaspoon crushed red pepper flakes

1/2 teaspoon black pepper

1/2 teaspoon dried Greek oregano

2 tablespoons finely chopped fresh cilantro (see headnote, page 74)

Score the steak on both sides with a very sharp knife.

Combine the herbs and spices, except the fresh cilantro, and rub into both sides of steak. Place in a shallow container and cover and refrigerate at least 4 hours or overnight.

Remove steak from refrigerator 1 hour before cooking. Prepare grill or broiler. Cook steak for about 3–5 minutes on each side, for rare to medium rare.

Slice the steak across the grain on a diagonal. Serve sprinkled with cilantro.

per serving

Calories	272	Cholesterol	85.9 mg
Protein	35 g	Calcium	22.3 mg
Carbohydrates	1.63 g	Iron	4.17 mg
Fat—Total	13.4 g	Sodium	1186 mg

three-peppered flank steak

The peppers and brown sugar combine to make a steak that is both spicy and sweet, a perfect combination that can be served hot, cold, or at room temperature.

serves 4

1 1/2 pounds flank or skirt steak, trimmed of fat

1/2–1 teaspoon crushed red pepper flakes

1/2 teaspoon black pepper

1/2 teaspoon white pepper

1 teaspoon kosher salt

1 teaspoon dried thyme

1 teaspoon brown sugar

Score the steak on both sides with a very sharp knife.

Combine the peppers, salt, thyme, and brown sugar and rub into both sides of steak. Place in a shallow container, cover and refrigerate at least 4 hours or overnight.

Remove steak from refrigerator 1 hour before cooking. Prepare grill or broiler. Cook steak for about 3–5 minutes on each side, for rare to medium rare.

Slice the steak across the grain on a diagonal.

per serving

Calories	265	Cholesterol	85.9 mg
Protein	34.6 g	Calcium	10.2 mg
Carbohydrates	.734 g	Iron	3.28 mg
Fat—Total	12.9 g	Sodium	639 mg

orange basil steak

1 1/2 pounds flank or skirt steak, trimmed of fat

1 tablespoon dried basil

2–3 garlic cloves, peeled and finely chopped

1 teaspoon black pepper

1/2 cup orange juice

1/4 cup red wine vinegar

1/4 cup chopped fresh basil leaves

Score the steak on both sides with a very sharp knife.

Combine the dried basil, garlic, black pepper, orange juice, and vinegar and pour over the steak in a shallow glass or ceramic container. Cover and refrigerate at least 4 hours or overnight, turning occasionally.

Remove steak from refrigerator 1 hour before cooking. Prepare grill or broiler. Remove steak from marinade; discard marinade. Cook steak for about 3–5 minutes on each side, for rare to medium rare.

Slice the steak across the grain on a diagonal and serve with fresh basil sprinkled on top.

per serving

Calories	282	Cholesterol	85.9 mg
Protein	35.1 g	Calcium	21.1 mg
Carbohydrates	4.86 g	Iron	3.53 mg
Fat—Total	13 g	Sodium	107 mg

orange mustard pork chops

A little sweet, a little tart, orange mustard pork chops are easy to prepare and easy to love.

serves 4

4 (7-ounce) center-cut pork chops

2 tablespoons grainy Dijon mustard

³/₄ cup orange juice

3 garlic cloves, peeled and finely chopped

Arrange the pork in one layer in a shallow glass or ceramic container. Combine the mustard, orange juice, and garlic cloves and pour over the pork. Cover and refrigerate at least 4 hours or overnight, turning occasionally.

Remove as much of the marinade as possible from the chops, and place it in a small saucepan. Bring to a boil over high heat and set aside.

Prepare grill or broiler. Place chops on a rack in a roasting pan. Cook for about 5 minutes on each side or until cooked through. Serve with reserved sauce.

per serving

Calories	344	Cholesterol	125 mg
Protein	44.6 g	Calcium	25.2 mg
Carbohydrates	5.91 g	Iron	1.94 mg
Fat—Total	14.7 g	Sodium	230 mg

oriental pork loin with garlic and ginger

1 1/4 pounds pork loin, thinly sliced

6 tablespoons soy sauce

2 tablespoons rice wine vinegar

4 garlic cloves, peeled and finely chopped or pressed

1 quarter-size slice of fresh gingerroot, finely chopped

1 teaspoon crushed red pepper flakes (optional)

2 scallions, including greens, sliced lengthwise

1/2 red bell pepper, seeded and thinly sliced

1/2–3/4 cup Chicken Stock (page 18) or low-sodium canned or from bouillon cube

Arrange pork in one layer in a shallow glass or ceramic container. Combine soy sauce, vinegar, garlic cloves, ginger, and crushed red pepper flakes and pour over pork. Cover and refrigerate no more than 4 hours, turning occasionally.

Heat a large cast-iron or nonstick skillet over medium heat, about 5 minutes or until a drop of water flicked on it bursts into droplets. Remove the pork from the marinade (reserve the marinade). Brown the pork on both sides and remove to a plate. Do not wash the pan. Add scallions and bell pepper and cook for about 5 minutes or until they start to brown. Add chicken broth and reserved marinade and bring to a boil. Add pork and cook about another 2 minutes or until just heated through.

per serving

Calories	331	Cholesterol	126 mg
Protein	41.6 g	Calcium	18.4 mg
Carbohydrates	3.91 g	Iron	1.87 mg
Fat—Total	15.8 g	Sodium	1613 mg

oriental pork with broccoli

The secret to dieting while keeping once-thought-to-be-fatty pork on your table is to buy the lower-fat variety and to eat small amounts. And, as in this dish, always pair pork with lots of fresh vegetables.

serves 4

1 (1-pound) thinly sliced boneless pork chop, cut into $1/4$-inch slices

3 tablespoons light soy sauce

2 tablespoons sherry vinegar or Japanese rice wine vinegar

$1/2$ teaspoon white sugar

4 teaspoons cornstarch

1 quarter-size slice of fresh gingerroot, peeled, if desired, and finely chopped

2–3 garlic cloves, peeled and finely chopped or pressed

$1/4$ teaspoon crushed red pepper flakes

1 large or 2 small heads broccoli, florets cut into walnut-size pieces and stems peeled and thinly sliced

1 red bell pepper, cored and thinly sliced

1-inch strip orange zest, julienned

1 tablespoon cold water

$1 1/4$ cups Chicken Stock (page 18) or low-sodium canned or from bouillon cubes

1 tablespoon dry sherry

2 tablespoons coarsely chopped fresh basil

Arrange pork in one layer in a shallow glass or ceramic container. Combine 2 tablespoons soy sauce, all the vinegar and sugar, and 2 teaspoons of the cornstarch and pour over pork. Cover and refrigerate 3 hours or overnight, turning occasionally. Heat a large nonstick skillet or wok over medium heat, add pork, and cook for about 2 minutes. Set pork aside and rinse pan. Return pan to heat and add ginger, garlic, and red pepper flakes. Cook for 2–3 minutes. Add broccoli, red pepper, and orange peel and stir until ingredients are thoroughly mixed. Cook 2 minutes.

Combine remaining 2 teaspoons cornstarch with water and set aside.

Add stock, sherry, and remaining 1 tablespoon soy sauce and bring to a boil. Gradually stir in cornstarch mixture and continue to stir until sauce becomes glossy, about 1 minute. Add reserved pork and cook about 2 minutes or until just heated through. Garnish with fresh basil and serve immediately.

per serving

Calories	243	Cholesterol	71.4 mg
Protein	29.6 g	Calcium	54.5 mg
Carbohydrates	10.4 g	Iron	2.17 mg
Fat—Total	8.91 g	Sodium	507 mg

mustard oregano pork loin

2 pounds pork loin, well trimmed and untied

1 1/2 cups red wine

2 tablespoons dried Greek oregano

2 tablespoons Dijon mustard

5 garlic cloves, peeled and finely chopped

Arrange the pork loin flat in a large shallow glass or ceramic container. Combine the wine, oregano, mustard, and garlic cloves and pour over the pork. Cover and refrigerate four hours or overnight, turning occasionally.

Preheat oven to 350 degrees. Take pork from refrigerator. Remove and reserve as much marinade as possible. Place the pork in a shallow roasting pan and bake for about 1 hour or until the internal temperature reaches 140 degrees. Brush with reserved marinade from time to time. Let the pork rest 10 minutes before serving.

per serving

Calories	395	Cholesterol	157 mg
Protein	56.3 g	Calcium	25.5 mg
Carbohydrates	2.01 g	Iron	3.45 mg
Fat—Total	9.9 g	Sodium	213 mg

pork with fennel

Pork with fennel is an Italian tradition, here improved with the addition of sambuca and the subtraction of olive oil. Serve with Garlic Mashed Potatoes (page 175) and Roasted Mixed Vegetables (page 191).

serves 4

$1/2$ cup Vegetable or Chicken Stock (page 17 and 18) or low-sodium canned or from bouillon cube

1 medium-size fennel bulb, thinly sliced

1 garlic clove, peeled and chopped

4 (6-ounce) boneless pork chops, pounded thin

2 tablespoons sambuca

Pepper to taste

Place stock and fennel in a nonstick skillet over medium heat; cover and cook 30 minutes. Remove and reserve pan contents.

Add garlic and pork to pan and brown pork over medium-high heat about 2–3 minutes on each side.

Add reserved fennel mixture and sambuca and cook about another 10 minutes or until the pork is cooked through. Add pepper to taste. Serve immediately.

per serving

Calories	412	Cholesterol	135 mg
Protein	40.9 g	Calcium	39.9 mg
Carbohydrates	7.72 g	Iron	1.81 mg
Fat—Total	22 g	Sodium	146 mg

sesame pork chops

serves 4

4 (6-ounce) pork cutlets, pounded thin

$1/2$ cup orange juice

1 tablespoon soy sauce

$1/4$ teaspoon cayenne pepper

1 teaspoon oriental sesame oil

1 teaspoon toasted sesame seeds

Heat a large cast-iron or nonstick skillet over medium-high heat, about 5 minutes or until a drop of water flicked on it bursts into droplets. Place pork cutlets in pan and cook about 4–5 minutes per side. Add remaining ingredients, except for the sesame seeds, and cook until heated through. Serve immediately, sprinkled with sesame seeds.

per serving

Calories	357	Cholesterol	121 mg
Protein	36.2 g	Calcium	20.1 mg
Carbohydrates	3.67 g	Iron	1.44 mg
Fat—Total	21.1 g	Sodium	353 mg

rosemary apple pork chops

4 (6-ounce) pork chops

1 teaspoon dried rosemary

$1/2$ cup apple juice concentrate

2 garlic cloves, peeled and finely chopped

Place pork chops in a shallow glass or ceramic container and cover with rosemary, apple juice concentrate, and garlic. Cover and refrigerate 4 hours or overnight, turning occasionally.

Take chops from refrigerator, remove as much of the marinade as possible, and place it in a small saucepan. Bring to a boil over high heat and set aside.

Prepare grill or broiler. Place chops on a rack and cook for about 5 minutes on each side, or until as well done as desired. Serve with sauce.

per serving

Calories	385	Cholesterol	121 mg
Protein	35.7 g	Calcium	16 mg
Carbohydrates	14.4 g	Iron	1.51 mg
Fat—Total	19.7 g	Sodium	104 mg

mustard veal chops

4 (6-ounce) veal chops, about 1 1/2 inches thick, trimmed of fat

4 tablespoons dry white wine

4 tablespoons Chicken Stock (page 18) or low-sodium canned or from bouillon cube

5 tablespoons Dijon mustard

2 teaspoons dried basil

Heat a large cast-iron or nonstick skillet over medium-high heat, about 5 minutes or until a drop of water flicked on it bursts into droplets. Place veal in pan and cook for about 4–5 minutes on the first side, about 3 minutes on the second. Remove veal from pan and set aside. Add remaining ingredients and bring to a boil over medium heat. Reduce heat to low, return veal to pan, and cook about another 2 minutes, or until veal is coated with sauce.

per serving

Calories	316	Cholesterol	160 mg
Protein	43.9 g	Calcium	59.2 mg
Carbohydrates	1.43 g	Iron	1.87 mg
Fat—Total	12.7 g	Sodium	357 mg

veal scallopine with tomato sauce

The classic Italian dish, scaled down.

1 Spanish onion, peeled and coarsely chopped

1 yellow or red bell pepper, seeded and coarsely chopped

4 garlic cloves, peeled and finely chopped

1 (16-ounce) can tomatoes, including liquid, chopped

$1/2$ teaspoon crushed red pepper flakes

$1 1/4$ pounds veal scallop or cutlet, pounded as thin as possible

$1/2$ cup dry white wine

Heat a large nonstick pan over medium heat and add onion, bell pepper, and garlic. Cook about 10 minutes or until the vegetables begin to soften. Reduce heat to low and add tomatoes and red pepper flakes and cook about 20 minutes. Remove sauce from pan and set aside. Increase heat to high and add veal. Cook for about 2–3 minutes on each side or until cooked through. Remove veal and deglaze the pan with the wine. Add the reserved sauce to the pan, heat it, and serve it over the veal.

per serving

Calories	300	Cholesterol	100 mg
Protein	27.3 g	Calcium	63.1 mg
Carbohydrates	8.67 g	Iron	1.86 mg
Fat—Total	15 g	Sodium	255 mg

veal saltimbocca

1 teaspoon olive oil

12 fresh sage leaves

3–4 cloves garlic, peeled and thinly sliced

4 (6-ounce) veal cutlets or scallops, pounded as thin as possible

1/4 cup shaved Parmesan cheese

1 tablespoon all-purpose white flour, for dusting veal

1/3 cup dry white wine

Heat a large skillet over medium-low heat and add oil. Heat oil and add sage. Cook 1 minute or until sage is beginning to brown.

Remove sage and set aside. Do not wash pan. Add garlic to pan and cook about 3–5 minutes or until golden. Set aside. Again, do not wash pan. Top each cutlet with 1 sage leaf and 1 tablespoon shaved Parmesan cheese. Fold over and lightly dust each cutlet with flour. Heat skillet over medium-high heat, about 3–5 minutes or until a drop of water flicked on it bursts into droplets. Place veal in pan and cook for about 2–3 minutes on each side. Remove veal and deglaze pan with the wine. Add reserved sage and garlic and bring to a boil over high heat, then reduce heat to low and simmer until slightly thickened. Serve immediately over veal.

per serving

Calories	421	Cholesterol	155 mg
Protein	41.4 g	Calcium	124 mg
Carbohydrates	1.88 g	Iron	1.61 mg
Fat—Total	25 g	Sodium	219 mg

pasta, rice, and pizza

pasta with roasted yellow peppers

This delicate sauce is a delicious change of pace for pasta eaters. And what could be easier?

serves 4

1 pound pasta of your choice

6 roasted yellow peppers (page 21), finely chopped or pureed

1/2 cup Chicken Stock (page 18) or low-sodium canned or from bouillon cube

Bring a 6- or 8-quart pot of salted water to a boil. Cook the pasta until *al dente*. Drain immediately.

While the pasta is cooking, combine the chopped or pureed peppers with the chicken stock. Pour over drained pasta and serve immediately.

per serving

Calories	500	Cholesterol	0 mg
Protein	17.9 g	Calcium	52.4 mg
Carbohydrates	102 g	Iron	5.72 mg
Fat—Total	2.56 g	Sodium	22.5 mg

pasta with mussels and tomatoes

The mussel lover's choice—long on mussels and short on fat.

1 small Spanish onion, peeled and coarsely chopped

3 garlic cloves, peeled and finely chopped

$1/2$ teaspoon dried thyme

1 (16-ounce) can whole tomatoes, drained and sliced

1 cup canned or fresh crushed tomatoes, including liquid

$1/2$ teaspoon crushed red pepper flakes

Salt to taste

1 cup dry white wine

48 mussels, bearded and scrubbed

1 pound pasta of your choice

Heat a large nonstick pan over medium heat and add onion, garlic, and thyme. Cook about 10 minutes or until the vegetables begin to soften.

Reduce the flame to low, add tomatoes and red pepper flakes, and simmer about 20 minutes. Salt to taste.

Remove sauce from pan and set aside but do not wash the pan. Use the same pan to bring the wine to a boil. Reduce flame to low and add mussels and cook until they open, about 2–4 minutes. Discard any mussels that don't open.

While the sauce cooks, bring a large pot of salted water to a boil. Cook the pasta until *al dente*.

Drain pasta and place in four separate bowls. Cover with sauce and top each with 12 mussels in the shell.

per serving

Calories	705	Cholesterol	63.6 mg
Protein	43.5 g	Calcium	119 mg
Carbohydrates	105 g	Iron	13.4 mg
Fat—Total	7.28 g	Sodium	776 mg

pasta with broccoli and sun-dried tomatoes

Sun-dried tomatoes and tomato paste give an additional burst of flavor to a traditional sauce.

serves 4

5 shallots, peeled and thinly sliced

3 garlic cloves, peeled and thinly sliced

1 head broccoli, stems julienned and florets chopped

8–10 sun-dried tomatoes, chopped

2 tablespoons sun-dried tomato paste

$^1/_2$ cup Chicken Stock (page 18) or low-sodium canned or from bouillon cube

1 pound pasta of your choice

Heat a large nonstick pan over medium heat and add shallots and garlic. Cook for about 10 minutes or until the vegetables begin to soften. Reduce heat to low and add broccoli, sun-dried tomatoes, sun-dried tomato paste, and chicken stock. Cook for about 10 minutes, or until the broccoli is *al dente*.

If desired, place in a food processor fitted with a steel blade and pulse until chunky.

While the sauce cooks, bring a large pot of salted water to a boil. Cook the pasta until *al dente*, then drain and add the broccoli mixture. Toss to combine.

per serving

Calories	518	Cholesterol	0 mg
Protein	23.8 g	Calcium	78.7 mg
Carbohydrates	96.5 g	Iron	6.43 mg
Fat—Total	4.04 g	Sodium	267 mg

baked pasta with roasted eggplant sauce

A wonderful side dish for 8, or serve it as an entree for 4.

1 medium eggplant

1 small onion, peeled and chopped

4 garlic cloves, peeled and finely chopped

1 small zucchini, halved lengthwise and sliced

2 fresh tomatoes, coarsely chopped

1 cup nonfat ricotta cheese

2 tablespoons dried basil

1 teaspoon ground nutmeg

1 pound medium-size pasta, such as shells or rotini

$1/4$ pound part-skim mozzarella cheese, shredded

Preheat oven to 450 degrees.

Prick eggplant all over with the tines of a fork, place in oven, and cook for about 45 minutes or until very soft. Set aside until cool enough to handle, peel, and finely chop.

Heat a large nonstick skillet over medium heat and add onion, garlic, and zucchini. Cook for about 15 minutes or until the vegetables begin to soften. Reduce heat to low, add eggplant and tomatoes, and cook about 10 minutes. Set aside.

Combine ricotta cheese with basil and nutmeg.

Bring a 6- or 8-quart pot of salted water to a boil. Cook the pasta until *al dente*. Drain, add ricotta mixture, and toss to combine.

Reduce the oven temperature to 350 degrees.

In an 8 × 12-inch glass or metal ovenproof pan, arrange half the pasta mixture, then half the eggplant mixture, then repeat. Sprinkle the top with mozzarella cheese. Bake about 45 minutes or until the top begins to brown.

per side dish serving

Calories	306	Cholesterol	7.64 mg
Protein	15.8 g	Calcium	224 mg
Carbohydrates	52.7 g	Iron	2.71 mg
Fat—Total	3.62 g	Sodium	134 mg

pasta with bolognese sauce

Traditional Bolognese sauce is not made with shiitake mushrooms but you'll find that they add a rich, beefy taste.

serves 8

$^1/_2$ red or Spanish onion, peeled and finely diced

1 celery stalk, finely diced

1 carrot, finely diced

1 pound ground turkey

1 cup dry white wine

1 cup skim milk

$^1/_4$ cup nonfat dry milk

1 (28-ounce) can chunky-style tomatoes, including liquid

1 cup finely chopped fresh shiitake mushrooms

2 tablespoons sun-dried tomato paste

$^1/_4$ teaspoon ground nutmeg

2 pounds pasta of your choice

Heat a large nonstick skillet over medium heat and add onion, celery, and carrot. Cook for about 15 minutes or until the vegetables begin to soften. Reduce heat to low and add turkey. Cook, all the while separating with a fork, about 5 minutes or until the turkey begins to brown.

Add the wine and the milk. Sprinkle the nonfat milk over the mixture, stirring constantly and cook over low heat about 5 minutes. Add tomatoes, mushrooms, sun-dried tomato paste, and nutmeg and cook, over very low heat, for 2–3 hours or until it reaches desired thickness.

Bring a large pot of salted water to a boil. Cook the pasta until *al dente*. Drain pasta, add the Bolognese sauce, and toss to combine.

per serving

Calories	599	Cholesterol	44.3 mg
Protein	29.5 g	Calcium	131 mg
Carbohydrates	96.8 g	Iron	6.2 mg
Fat—Total	7.84 g	Sodium	285 mg

pasta fagioli

While Canadian bacon isn't usually included in diet meals, the small amount here adds so much flavor, and so little fat, and so few calories that it would be a sin to do without it.

serves 4

2 ounces Canadian bacon, chopped

6 cups Chicken or Vegetable Stock (pages 18 or 17) or low-sodium canned or from bouillon cubes

1 Spanish onion, peeled and chopped

2 celery stalks, chopped

2 carrots, chopped

2 garlic cloves, peeled and finely chopped

1 quarter-size slice of fresh gingerroot, peeled if desired, and chopped

$1/4$ teaspoon crushed red pepper flakes

1 teaspoon dried rosemary

1 (28-ounce) can chunk-style tomatoes, including liquid

2 (20-ounce) cans cannellini beans, drained and rinsed

1 cup small pasta, such as elbows

Cook bacon in a 6- or 8-quart stockpot over medium-low heat until all fat is rendered. Discard fat and reserve bacon. In the same pan, combine $1/2$ cup chicken stock, the onion, celery, carrots, garlic, and ginger, and cook over medium-low heat until vegetables are tender, about 20 minutes.

Add crushed red pepper flakes, rosemary, tomatoes, and remaining stock and simmer for 1 hour.

Add beans and cook for an additional 20 minutes.

While the beans are cooking, bring a large pot of salted water to a boil. Cook the pasta until *al dente*, drain and add to pot.

per serving

Calories	518	Cholesterol	7.09 mg
Protein	36 g	Calcium	285 mg
Carbohydrates	85.3 g	Iron	11 mg
Fat—Total	4.86 g	Sodium	675 mg

pasta with artichokes and mushrooms

Pasta Italiano for the gourmet!

1 small onion, peeled and thinly sliced

4–6 garlic cloves, peeled and chopped

1 cup chopped fresh shiitake mushrooms

1 (16-ounce) can artichoke bottoms packed in water, drained, rinsed, and thinly sliced

1 (16-ounce) can artichoke hearts packed in water, drained, rinsed, and quartered

2 fresh tomatoes, chopped

1 cup Chicken Stock (page 18) or low-sodium canned or from bouillon cube

$1/2$ cup dry white wine

1 pound pasta of your choice

Heat a large nonstick pan over medium heat and add onion, garlic, and shiitake mushrooms. Cook about 10 minutes or until the vegetables begin to soften. Reduce heat to low and add artichoke bottoms, artichoke hearts, tomatoes, chicken stock, and white wine and cook for about 30 minutes.

If desired, place in a food processor fitted with a steel blade and pulse until chunky.

While the sauce cooks, bring a large pot of salted water to a boil. Cook the pasta until *al dente*, then drain and add the artichoke mixture. Toss to combine.

per serving

Calories	513	Cholesterol	0 mg
Protein	18.7 g	Calcium	44.3 mg
Carbohydrates	99.6 g	Iron	5.38 mg
Fat—Total	2.74 g	Sodium	64.8 mg

pasta with tomato, artichokes, shrimp, and feta cheese

serves 4

3 garlic cloves, peeled and finely chopped

3 fresh tomatoes, chopped

1 teaspoon dried basil

1 (16-ounce) can artichoke hearts in water, drained and quartered

2 teaspoons dried Greek oregano

2 cups Chicken Stock (page 18) or low-sodium canned or from bouillon cubes

$1/4$ cup red wine

$1/2$ pound shrimp, shelled and deveined

1 pound medium-size pasta, such as shells or rotini

$1/4$ cup fresh lemon juice (about 1 lemon)

$1/4$ cup chopped feta cheese

Heat a large nonstick skillet over high heat and add garlic, tomatoes, basil, artichoke hearts, and oregano. Bring to a boil over high heat. Add chicken stock and wine and return to a boil. Cook for about 2 minutes and add shrimp. Cook for about 3 minutes or until shrimp turns pink.

While sauce is cooking, bring a large pot of salted water to a boil. Cook the pasta until *al dente*. Drain and add to skillet with shrimp. At the last minute, add lemon juice and feta cheese and serve immediately.

per serving

Calories	568	Cholesterol	96.6 mg
Protein	29.7 g	Calcium	130 mg
Carbohydrates	94.2 g	Iron	6.69 mg
Fat—Total	6.71 g	Sodium	334 mg

pasta with fresh tomatoes

Is this dish pasta with fresh tomatoes or fresh tomatoes with pasta? Whichever way you decide, fresh tomatoes, fresh basil, and cooled pasta are perfect on a hot summer night.

serves 4

4 large beefsteak tomatoes, cubed

$^1/_2$ red onion, peeled and coarsely chopped

4 garlic cloves, peeled and finely chopped or crushed

$^1/_3$ – $^1/_2$ cup chopped fresh basil

2 tablespoons balsamic vinegar

$^1/_4$ teaspoon black pepper

$^1/_2$ pound medium-size pasta, such as shells or rotini

$^1/_2$ teaspoon salt

Combine tomatoes, onion, garlic, basil, balsamic vinegar, and pepper in a large bowl. Cover and refrigerate at least 4 hours or overnight.

Bring a large pot of salted water to a boil. Cook the pasta until *al dente*.

Drain, rinse, and cool to room temperature. Stir pasta into tomato mixture and add salt.

per serving

Calories	248	Cholesterol	0 mg
Protein	8.71 g	Calcium	22.1 mg
Carbohydrates	50.9 g	Iron	2.98 mg
Fat—Total	1.44 g	Sodium	285 mg

pasta with broccoli rabe and white beans

This combination of buttery white beans and bitter broccoli rabe creates a taste sensation so great you'll be tempted to eat this cold as well as hot.

serves 4

3 shallots, peeled and coarsely chopped

3 garlic cloves, peeled and finely chopped

1 head broccoli rabe, woody stems removed and coarsely chopped

2 cups cooked white beans (about ³/₄ cup dried; see Note, page 35)

2 cups Chicken Stock (page 18) or low-sodium canned or from bouillon cubes

¹/₄–¹/₂ teaspoon crushed red pepper flakes

1 cup drained, chopped, fresh or canned tomatoes

3 cups medium-size pasta, such as rotini or shells

Heat a large nonstick skillet over medium heat and add shallots and garlic. Cook for about 5 minutes or until the garlic begins to turn golden.

Add broccoli rabe and cook for 10 minutes. Add remaining ingredients, except pasta, and cook for 20 more minutes.

While the sauce is cooking, bring a large pot of salted water to a boil. Cook the pasta until *al dente.* Drain pasta and add it to the sauce.

per serving

Calories	398	Cholesterol	0 mg
Protein	20.9 g	Calcium	129 mg
Carbohydrates	74.5 g	Iron	6.59 mg
Fat—Total	2.44 g	Sodium	63.1 mg

linguine with spinach and garlic

$^1\!/_2$ pound linguine or spaghetti

2 teaspoons olive oil

3 garlic cloves, peeled and thinly sliced or finely chopped

1 pound fresh spinach; remove stems and coarsely chop leaves

Bring a large pot of salted water to a boil. Cook the pasta just until *al dente*.

Meanwhile, heat a large skillet over medium heat and add olive oil. Add garlic and cook about 5 minutes or until golden. When pasta is almost ready, add spinach to its pot. Continue to boil 2 minutes. Remove pasta and spinach with tongs or slotted spoon and add to pan with garlic. Serve immediately.

per serving

Calories	255	Cholesterol	0 mg
Protein	10.5 g	Calcium	122 mg
Carbohydrates	46.3 g	Iron	5.27 mg
Fat—Total	3.54 g	Sodium	93.5 mg

linguine giovanni

This herb-filled pasta dish is sure to be a favorite.

serves 4

3 garlic cloves, peeled and finely chopped or crushed

$1/4$ cup water, Chicken or Vegetable Stock (page 18 or page 17) or low-sodium canned or from bouillon cube

$1/2$ teaspoon crushed red pepper flakes

$1/2$ pound linguine

3–4 beefsteak tomatoes, cored and diced

$1/2$ cup coarsely chopped fresh flat-leaf parsley

$1/2$ cup coarsely chopped fresh basil

$1/8$ cup finely chopped fresh chives

2 tablespoons grated Parmesan cheese

Salt and pepper to taste

Place garlic, water or stock, and red pepper flakes in a large skillet and bring to a boil over high heat. Reduce heat to medium and cook about 3–5 minutes or until garlic is translucent.

Bring a large pot of salted water to a boil. Cook the pasta until *al dente*. Remove $1/4$ cup pasta liquid and add to garlic pan. Drain pasta and set it aside.

Add tomatoes and herbs to garlic and cook another 2 minutes.

Transfer drained pasta to skillet and cook until heated through. Sprinkle Parmesan cheese and season with salt and pepper. Serve immediately.

per serving

Calories	253	Cholesterol	2.46 mg
Protein	10.1 g	Calcium	77.7 mg
Carbohydrates	48.2 g	Iron	3.37 mg
Fat—Total	2.37 g	Sodium	80.7 mg

lasagna

Lasagna always tops the list of family favorites. This new recipe combines low fat and high flavor.

serves 4 with leftovers

¹/₂ pound skim-milk ricotta

¹/₂ cup skim milk

1 tablespoon dried basil

¹/₃ pound skim-milk mozzarella cheese, grated

1 tablespoon grated Romano cheese

1 tablespoon grated Parmesan cheese

¹/₂ pound lasagna noodles

2¹/₂ cups tomato sauce (use Shiitake Mushroom and Tomato Sauce [page 47], Tomato Sauce with Sweet Peppers and Hot and Sweet Sausages [page 48], or Classic Meat Sauce [page 49], or store-bought)

Preheat oven to 350 degrees.

Combine ricotta, skim milk, and basil in a small mixing bowl. Set aside.

Combine mozzarella, Romano, and Parmesan cheeses in another small mixing bowl and set aside.

Bring a large pot of salted water to a boil. Cook the lasagna noodles until *al dente*. Drain.

Place ¹/₂ cup sauce in the bottom of a 9 × 12-inch ovenproof pan. Cover with 3 lasagna noodles. Cover noodles with half the ricotta mixture and then 1 cup of the sauce. Repeat. Top with mozzarella mixture. Cover with aluminum foil, place in oven, and bake for 30 minutes. Remove foil and bake for an additional 30 minutes or until golden on top.

per serving

Calories	370	Cholesterol	32.8 mg
Protein	22.6 g	Calcium	428 mg
Carbohydrates	47.2 g	Iron	3 mg
Fat—Total	10.4 g	Sodium	1008 mg

fennel and orange risotto

This unusual combination of fennel and orange will have your guests applauding as well as guessing.

serves 4

1/2 red onion, peeled and finely chopped

I medium-size fennel bulb, finely diced, I tablespoon fernlike tops reserved

3 garlic cloves, peeled and finely chopped or crushed

4 cups Chicken or Vegetable Stock (page 18 or 17) or low-sodium canned or from bouillon cubes

1 1/2 cups uncooked Arborio rice

1/2 cup dry white wine

I teaspoon freshly grated orange zest

2 tablespoons sambuca or Pernod

Combine onion, fennel, garlic, and ½ cup chicken stock in a large skillet and cook over medium-low heat until fennel is soft, about 15 minutes.

Add rice and stir until completely combined.

Raise heat to medium and add white wine very slowly, stirring all the while.

Add the remaining chicken stock gradually, ½ cup at a time. Allow each addition of the stock to be absorbed into the rice mixture before adding the next. This will take about 15–20 minutes. Add orange zest, reserved fernlike tops, and sambuca, and serve immediately.

per serving

Calories	361	Cholesterol	0 mg
Protein	10.7 g	Calcium	63.9 mg
Carbohydrates	64.9 g	Iron	4.07 mg
Fat—Total	2.07 g	Sodium	108 mg

artichoke risotto

By not sautéing the vegetables in butter, almost all the fat is removed—and literally none of the flavor. Not only does this put risotto on the dieter's plate, but it tastes so rich that one can hardly imagine cooking it any other way.

serves 4

3 garlic cloves, peeled and finely chopped or crushed

4 cups Chicken Stock or more if necessary (page 18) or low-sodium canned or from bouillon cubes

1 1/2 cups uncooked Arborio rice

1 cup dry white wine

10 cherry tomatoes, quartered

1 (20-ounce) can artichoke bottoms in water, drained, rinsed, and chopped

2 teaspoons chopped fresh mint

Combine garlic and 1/4 cup chicken stock in a large skillet and cook over medium-low heat until garlic is soft, about 15 minutes.

Add rice and stir until thoroughly combined.

Raise heat to medium and add white wine very slowly, stirring all the while. When the wine is completely absorbed into the mixture, add the tomatoes and artichokes and stir until completely combined.

Add the remaining chicken stock gradually, 1/2 cup at a time. Allow each addition of the stock to be absorbed into the rice mixture before adding the next. This will take about 15–20 minutes. Add fresh mint and serve immediately.

per serving

Calories	392	Cholesterol	0 mg
Protein	13.7 g	Calcium	60.3 mg
Carbohydrates	68.9 g	Iron	4.51 mg
Fat—Total	2.6 g	Sodium	142 mg

tomato and zucchini pizza

Once you master this, you can make all sorts of substitutions, adding and subtracting cheeses, vegetables, meats, whatever your fancy.

serves 4

Olive oil cooking spray

Cornmeal

12 ounces pizza dough, homemade or store-bought (see Note)

$1/4$ cup tomato sauce (use Shiitake Mushroom and Tomato Sauce [page 47], Tomato Sauce with Sweet Peppers and Hot and Sweet Sausages [page 48], or Classic Meat Sauce [page 49], or store-bought)

$1/4$ cup nonfat ricotta cheese

$1/3$ cup shredded skim-milk mozzarella cheese

1 medium-size zucchini, thinly sliced (about 1 cup)

1 cup chopped fresh tomatoes

Preheat oven to 500 degrees. Lightly coat a pizza pan with olive oil cooking spray and sprinkle with cornmeal.

Roll out the pizza dough to the size of your pan (anywhere from 12 to 16 inches), place it on the pan, and spread the tomato sauce all over it. Dot with the ricotta cheese and then sprinkle with mozzarella. Arrange the zucchini slices in a circle around the edge of the dough and sprinkle with the tomatoes.

Bake for about 7–10 minutes or until pizza is bubbling and the crust is brown.

NOTE:

Most pizza shops will sell dough. Most grocery stores sell frozen and prepared dough.

per serving

Calories	284	Cholesterol	5.02 mg
Protein	12.3 g	Calcium	234 mg
Carbohydrates	47.3 g	Iron	2.9 mg
Fat—Total	5.15 g	Sodium	570 mg

pizza with roasted vegetables and mozzarella

Olive oil cooking spray

Cornmeal

12 ounces pizza dough, homemade or store-bought (see Note, page 155)

1 recipe Roasted Mixed Vegetables (page 191)

¼ cup shredded skim-milk mozzarella cheese

Preheat oven to 500 degrees. Lightly coat a pizza pan with olive oil cooking spray and sprinkle with cornmeal.

Roll out the pizza dough to the size of your pan (anywhere from 12 to 16 inches), place it on the pan, and top with the roasted vegetables. Sprinkle with the mozzarella cheese and bake for about 7–10 minutes or until the pizza is bubbling and the crust is brown.

per serving

Calories	290	Cholesterol	3.81 mg
Protein	10.7 g	Calcium	184 mg
Carbohydrates	51.6 g	Iron	3.19 mg
Fat—Total	4.88 g	Sodium	572 mg

pizza with spinach and feta cheese

Olive oil cooking spray

Cornmeal

12 ounces pizza dough, homemade or store-bought (see Note, page 155)

$^1/_4$ cup nonfat ricotta cheese

1 (10-ounce) bag fresh spinach, stems removed, washed and thoroughly dried

$^1/_3$ cup crumbled feta cheese

Preheat oven to 500 degrees. Lightly coat a pizza pan with olive oil cooking spray and sprinkle with cornmeal.

Roll out the pizza dough to the size of your pan (anywhere from 12 to 16 inches), arrange it on the pan, and spread with the ricotta cheese. Cover the cheese with the spinach and sprinkle with feta cheese. Bake for about 7–10 minutes or until the pizza is bubbling and the crust is brown.

per serving

Calories	309	Cholesterol	18.1 mg
Protein	13.7 g	Calcium	326 mg
Carbohydrates	46.2 g	Iron	4.47 mg
Fat—Total	7.91 g	Sodium	705 mg

vegetables

asparagus with anchovies, garlic, and lemon

¹/₂ cup water

1 pound asparagus, woody stems discarded, remainder cut into thirds

1 teaspoon olive oil

3 garlic cloves, peeled and finely chopped

1–2 teaspoons anchovy paste

1 tablespoon lemon juice

Pepper to taste

Place water and asparagus in a skillet and bring to a boil. Boil until there is no liquid left, or until asparagus is *al dente*. Set aside. In the same skillet, heat the olive oil, add the garlic and anchovy paste, and mash with a wooden spoon. Add the reserved asparagus and mix until coated. Add the lemon juice and add pepper to taste.

Serve immediately.

per serving

Calories	38.1	Cholesterol	.85 mg
Protein	2.88 g	Calcium	26.2 mg
Carbohydrates	5.16 g	Iron	1.04 mg
Fat—Total	1.45 g	Sodium	38.9 mg

asparagus with shallots

3 garlic cloves, peeled and finely chopped

2 shallots, peeled and coarsely chopped

1 pound asparagus, woody stems discarded, remainder cut into thirds

1/4 cup Chicken or Vegetable Stock (page 18 or 17) or low-sodium canned or from bouillon cube

Heat a large nonstick skillet over medium heat and add garlic and shallots. Cook for about 5 minutes or until the vegetables begin turning golden. Increase heat to high, add asparagus, and cook about 2 minutes or until asparagus begins to brown. Add chicken broth and cook 1 more minute.

per serving

Calories	35.7	Cholesterol	0 mg
Protein	3.14 g	Calcium	28.2 mg
Carbohydrates	6.9 g	Iron	1.14 mg
Fat—Total	.327 g	Sodium	7.97 mg

roasted beets

You'll never turn your nose up at beets again once you've tried these; roasting brings out their richness, sweetness, and depth. They're sure to become favorites.

serves 4

3 large beets (about 1 pound, excluding greens)

$1/2$ cup water, Chicken or Vegetable Stock (page 18 or 17), or low-sodium canned or from bouillon cube

$1 1/2$ teaspoons balsamic vinegar

1 tablespoon finely chopped fresh dill

Preheat oven to 450 degrees.

Scrub beets and place in a medium-size baking pan with water or stock. Bake for 45 minutes or until tender when pierced with a fork.

When the beets are cool enough to handle, remove skins and slice thin. Add vinegar. Sprinkle with dill just prior to serving. Serve hot, at room temperature, or chilled.

per serving

Calories	53.8	Cholesterol	0 mg
Protein	2.44 g	Calcium	19.5 mg
Carbohydrates	11.1 g	Iron	.979 mg
Fat—Total	.373 g	Sodium	97.4 mg

broccoli with anchovies

When anchovies are paired with broccoli, you get quite a taste sensation.

4 garlic cloves, peeled and chopped or crushed

2 anchovy fillets

I small head broccoli, florets separated and stems peeled

Heat a large nonstick skillet over medium heat and add garlic. Cook for about 5 minutes or until golden. Add anchovies and stir until heated.

Bring a large pot of salted water to a boil. Cook broccoli until *al dente*, about 3–5 minutes. Drain and add stems to anchovy mixture. Cook 2 minutes, then add florets and cook 2 more minutes.

per serving

Calories	16.5	Cholesterol	1.7 mg
Protein	1.89 g	Calcium	25.7 mg
Carbohydrates	2.31 g	Iron	.48 mg
Fat—Total	.348 g	Sodium	85.2 mg

spicy brussels sprouts

1 cup water

1 (10-ounce) container fresh brussels sprouts, stems trimmed and marked with an X at bottom

3 garlic cloves, peeled and finely chopped

1 quarter-size slice of fresh gingerroot, peeled, if desired, and finely chopped

1–2 tablespoons light soy sauce

$^1/_2$ cup Chicken or Vegetable Stock (page 18 or 17), or low-sodium canned or from bouillon cube

$^1/_4$–$^1/_2$ crushed red pepper flakes

Bring water to a boil in a medium-size saucepan. Add brussels sprouts and cover. Cook for about 6 minutes, or until *al dente*. Cut in half through the stem.

Heat a large nonstick skillet over high heat and add garlic and ginger. Cook about 2 minutes or until they start to color. Add brussels sprouts and cook for about 2 more minutes. Add soy sauce, chicken stock, and red pepper flakes and cook about 5–7 minutes or until all the liquid has been absorbed.

per serving

Calories	37	Cholesterol	0 mg
Protein	3.17 g	Calcium	31.6 mg
Carbohydrates	6.75 g	Iron	1.12 mg
Fat—Total	.395 g	Sodium	219 mg

chinese cabbage

Reminiscent of dishes found in Chinese restaurants, this sweet-and-sour dish is equally good hot or cold.

serves 4

1 small head Chinese cabbage, thinly sliced

1 teaspoon powdered ginger

2–3 teaspoons oriental sesame oil

$^1/_2$–1 teaspoon salt

1–2 teaspoons white sugar or white sugar substitute

1–2 tablespoons soy sauce

$^1/_4$ cup fresh lemon juice

Black pepper to taste

Heat a large nonstick skillet over high heat, add cabbage, and cook it until it wilts, about 2–3 minutes. Add ginger, sesame oil, salt, and sugar and cook for about 1 minute. Remove from heat and add soy sauce, lemon juice, and pepper. Serve immediately or refrigerate and serve chilled.

per serving

Calories	47.6	Cholesterol	0 mg
Protein	1.46 g	Calcium	76 mg
Carbohydrates	4.98 g	Iron	.703 mg
Fat—Total	3 g	Sodium	697 mg

carrots with ginger

The taste and the scent of India come to carrots when they are cooked with ginger and cardamom.

serves 4

2 tablespoons water plus $1/2$ cup

2 garlic cloves, peeled and finely chopped

1 tablespoon finely chopped fresh gingerroot

1 pound carrots, peeled and thinly sliced at an angle

$1/8$ teaspoon ground cardamom

2 tablespoons balsamic vinegar

1 teaspoon brown sugar or brown sugar substitute

Place 2 tablespoons water, garlic, and ginger in a large nonstick pan and cook over medium heat for about 10 minutes or until garlic is soft. Increase heat to high, add carrots and remaining water, and cook for about 7 minutes or until water has evaporated and carrots begin to brown. Add cardamom, balsamic vinegar, and sugar and cook 2 more minutes.

per serving

Calories	58.4	Cholesterol	0 mg
Protein	1.17 g	Calcium	32.9 mg
Carbohydrates	14.1 g	Iron	.655 mg
Fat—Total	.216 g	Sodium	40.6 mg

grilled corn with curry and lime

2 tablespoons low-fat mayonnaise

2 tablespoons fresh lime juice

1 ¹/₂ teaspoons curry powder or more, to taste

Salt to taste

4 ears corn, husked and cleaned of the silk (see Note)

Prepare grill.

Mix together mayonnaise, lime juice, and curry powder in a small glass or ceramic bowl. Add salt to taste and set aside.

Place corn on grill and turn occasionally until corn is cooked, about 12 minutes.

Remove corn from grill and brush with curry and lime mixture.

NOTE:

You can also cook the corn in its husk, but first remove all the silk.

per serving

Calories	105	Cholesterol	1.87 mg
Protein	2.65 g	Calcium	2.92 mg
Carbohydrates	21.9 g	Iron	.475 mg
Fat—Total	2.5 g	Sodium	52 mg

oriental eggplant

This recipe transports eggplant from the ordinary to the sublime.

serves 4

1 medium-size eggplant

Salt

1 garlic clove, peeled and finely chopped

1 quarter-size slice of fresh gingerroot, peeled, if desired, and finely chopped

1/2 cup Chicken Stock (page 18) or low-sodium canned or from bouillon cube

2 tablespoons soy sauce

1 tablespoon rice vinegar

1/2 teaspoon cornstarch

1/2 teaspoon Chinese chili paste

Slice the eggplant as thin as possible, sprinkle with salt, and place in a colander over a plate or bowl. Let drain at least 1 hour. Rinse with cold water and pat dry with paper towels.

Heat a large nonstick skillet over medium heat and cook eggplant slices until lightly toasted on both sides. Remove and set aside.

Return the pan to medium heat, add garlic and ginger, and cook about 5 minutes or until golden. Add remaining ingredients, including reserved eggplant, and cook about 10 minutes or until almost all the liquid has been absorbed and eggplant has softened.

per serving

Calories	49.8	Cholesterol	0 mg
Protein	2.2 g	Calcium	11.2 mg
Carbohydrates	10.4 g	Iron	.744 mg
Fat—Total	.529 g	Sodium	533 mg

eggplant and peppers hoisin

The hoisin sauce and honey add a touch of sweetness to this slightly spicy dish.

serves 4

1 teaspoon canola oil

1 teaspoon oriental sesame oil

1 medium-size Japanese eggplant, quartered lengthwise

1 red bell pepper, seeded and sliced

1 yellow bell pepper, seeded and sliced

2 tablespoons plus 2 teaspoons cold water

2 teaspoons cornstarch

2 tablespoons soy sauce

2 tablespoons hoisin sauce

1 tablespoon honey

$1/4$ teaspoon cayenne pepper

Pinch salt

Heat canola and sesame oils in a wok over high heat. Add eggplant, bell peppers, and 2 tablespoons water and cook until vegetables are slightly tender, stirring occasionally.

Combine 2 teaspoons of cold water and cornstarch and set aside.

Add remaining ingredients to wok and bring to a boil. Gradually stir in cornstarch mixture. Stir until thickened.

per serving

Calories	109	Cholesterol	0 mg
Protein	2.45 g	Calcium	18.7 mg
Carbohydrates	20.3 g	Iron	1.04 mg
Fat—Total	3.1 g	Sodium	602 mg

trio of wild mushrooms

Perfect to serve with grilled steak or roasted chicken, these mushrooms are pure heaven.

$1/2$ pound fresh shiitake mushrooms, trimmed and wiped clean (don't substitute dried mushrooms)

$1/2$ pound fresh cremini mushrooms, trimmed and wiped clean

$1/2$ pound fresh button mushrooms, trimmed and wiped clean

2 teaspoons dried Greek oregano

$1 1/2$ teaspoons dried basil

2 garlic cloves, peeled and chopped

$1/4$ cup dry white wine, water, Chicken or Vegetable Stock (page 18 or 17), or low-sodium canned or from bouillon cube

1 tablespoon fresh lemon juice

Salt and pepper to taste

Preheat oven to 400 degrees.

Place mushrooms in one layer in a shallow roasting pan. Combine herbs, garlic, and wine in a smal bowl and pour over mushrooms. Bake about 20 minutes or until darkened.

Sprinkle with lemon juice and add salt and pepper to taste.

per serving

Calories	70.5	Cholesterol	0 mg
Protein	3.28 g	Calcium	8.96 mg
Carbohydrates	13.8 g	Iron	1.71 mg
Fat—Total	.606 g	Sodium	7.58 mg

balsamic onions

Try these sweet onions as a side dish with a simple grilled chicken, beef, or fish dish. The brave might even want to try them over plain pasta or as a pizza topping.

serves 4

Olive oil cooking spray

4 shallots, peeled and quartered

4 garlic cloves, peeled and chopped

2 Spanish onions, peeled and roughly chopped

2 red onions, peeled and roughly chopped

1 tablespoon brown sugar

2 tablespoons balsamic vinegar

1 teaspoon salt

Preheat oven to 450 degrees. Lightly coat a shallow roasting pan with cooking spray. In it, arrange shallots, garlic, and onions in a single layer.

Combine brown sugar, balsamic vinegar, and salt in a small bowl and pour over vegetables. Bake about 25 minutes or until browned.

per serving

Calories	58.7	Cholesterol	0 mg
Protein	1.62 g	Calcium	32.6 mg
Carbohydrates	13.6 g	Iron	.573 mg
Fat—Total	.244 g	Sodium	538 mg

oven-roasted potatoes with rosemary

French fries without the frying, these potatoes can be eaten as is or served with tomato ketchup. Try them for breakfast, as well as dinner.

serves 4

Olive oil cooking spray

12 red new potatoes, scrubbed, patted dry, and quartered

1 tablespoon dried rosemary

Preheat oven to 400 degrees. Lightly coat a shallow roasting pan with cooking spray.

Arrange potatoes and rosemary in pan and lightly spray with oil. Bake for about 45 minutes or until browned.

per serving

Calories	65.5	Cholesterol	0 mg
Protein	1.48 g	Calcium	5.25 mg
Carbohydrates	14.3 g	Iron	1.32 mg
Fat—Total	.502 g	Sodium	273 mg

lemon garlic french fries

A welcome variation for the no-fry potato fan.

serves 4

Olive oil cooking spray

3 large Russet potatoes, scrubbed and patted dry and cut lengthwise in 8 pieces

$^1/_4$ cup fresh lemon juice (about 1 lemon)

2 garlic cloves, peeled and chopped

2 teaspoons salt

Preheat oven to 375 degrees. Lightly coat a shallow roasting pan with cooking spray. In it, arrange potatoes in one layer. Combine lemon juice, garlic, and salt and pour over potatoes. Bake for about 45 minutes or until golden brown.

per serving

Calories	171	Cholesterol	0 mg
Protein	3.55 g	Calcium	17.5 mg
Carbohydrates	39.5 g	Iron	2.07 mg
Fat—Total	.453 g	Sodium	1078 mg

garlic mashed potatoes

You probably never thought you'd be eating mashed potatoes again. Yet here they are, low in fat and calories, jazzier than ever.

serves 4

8 small new potatoes, scrubbed or peeled, and quartered

3 garlic cloves, peeled

3 tablespoons Yogurt Cheese (page 19)

$3/4$ teaspoon kosher salt

$1/4$ teaspoon white pepper

2 tablespoons skim milk

1 tablespoon grated Parmesan cheese

Place potatoes and garlic in a medium-size saucepan and cover with water. Bring to a boil over high heat. Reduce heat to medium and cook for about 20 minutes or until potatoes are tender. Drain. Remove garlic. Mash it well with a fork. Add potatoes to mashed garlic and mash them with the fork. If you prefer your mashed potatoes smooth, use a hand beater. Do not use a food processor or blender; it will make the potatoes elastic. Add remaining ingredients. If necessary, reheat over low heat.

per serving

Calories	63.1	Cholesterol	2.55 mg
Protein	3 g	Calcium	71.4 mg
Carbohydrates	10.9 g	Iron	.912 mg
Fat—Total	.938 g	Sodium	624 mg

mashed sweet potatoes

3 medium-size sweet potatoes, scrubbed or peeled and quartered

2 garlic cloves, peeled and finely chopped or pressed

1 teaspoon chopped fresh gingerroot or more, to taste

3 tablespoons Yogurt Cheese (page 19)

$^3/_4$ teaspoon kosher salt

$^1/_4$ teaspoon white pepper

2 tablespoons skim milk

Place sweet potatoes, garlic, and ginger in a medium-size saucepan and cover with water. Bring to a boil over high heat. Reduce heat to medium and cook for about 20 minutes or until potatoes are tender. Drain and mash well with a fork. If you prefer your mashed potatoes smooth, use a hand beater. Do not use a food processor or blender; it will make the potatoes elastic. Add remaining ingredients. If necessary, reheat over low heat.

per serving

Calories	102	Cholesterol	1.32 mg
Protein	2.84 g	Calcium	70.4 mg
Carbohydrates	22.1 g	Iron	.4 mg
Fat—Total	.416 g	Sodium	422 mg

red potatoes with fennel and onions

Serve this with your favorite roasted chicken for a delicious and easy winter meal.

serves 4

Olive oil cooking spray

8 red new potatoes, scrubbed, patted dry, and quartered

1 fennel bulb, cut in large dice

2 red onions, peeled and cut into eighths

1 teaspoon kosher salt

$^1/_4$ teaspoon black pepper

Preheat oven to 450 degrees. Lightly coat a baking sheet with cooking spray.

Arrange potatoes, fennel, and onions on the baking sheet, season with salt and pepper, and bake for about 45 minutes or until the onions are browned.

per serving

Calories	81.3	Cholesterol	0 mg
Protein	2.37 g	Calcium	46.6 mg
Carbohydrates	17.8 g	Iron	1.51 mg
Fat—Total	.688 g	Sodium	746 mg

overstuffed broccoli and ricotta potatoes

These potatoes and a green salad form a complete meal.

4 Idaho potatoes, scrubbed and patted dry

1 branch broccoli, woody stem discarded, remaining stem julienned, florets chopped

1 scallion, including greens, chopped

1 teaspoon Dijon mustard

$^1/_2$ cup nonfat sour cream

$^1/_2$ cup skim-milk ricotta cheese

$^1/_2$ teaspoon salt

Pinch cayenne pepper

Preheat oven to 450 degrees.

Prick potatoes all over with the tines of a fork and place in oven. Bake for about 45 minutes or until tender. Slice top quarter off potatoes and remove flesh from both parts. Discard top skins. Mash flesh with a fork and add remaining ingredients. Divide into four parts and fill potato skins. Return to oven and cook about 10 minutes or until heated through and golden brown on top.

per serving

Calories	290	Cholesterol	9.48 mg
Protein	11.1 g	Calcium	120 mg
Carbohydrates	57.2 g	Iron	3.18 mg
Fat—Total	2.81 g	Sodium	365 mg

overstuffed blue potatoes

A tangy and filling treat for potato lovers.

4 Idaho potatoes, scrubbed and patted dry

4 tablespoons nonfat cream cheese

I tablespoon plus I teaspoon blue or Roquefort cheese

I teaspoon salt

$^1/_2$ cup low-fat buttermilk

Preheat oven to 450 degrees.

Prick potatoes all over with the tines of a fork and place in oven. Bake for about 45 minutes or until tender. Slice top quarter off potatoes and discard. Remove and reserve flesh from remaining portions. Mash with a fork and add remaining ingredients. Divide into four parts and stuff skins. Return to oven and cook about 10 minutes or until heated through and golden brown on top.

per serving

Calories	264	Cholesterol	7.62 mg
Protein	10.1 g	Calcium	65.7 mg
Carbohydrates	53.4 g	Iron	2.77 mg
Fat—Total	1.03 g	Sodium	783 mg

overstuffed salsa potatoes

These potatoes will return your bite with one of their own.

4 Idaho potatoes, scrubbed and patted dry

2 garlic cloves, peeled and finely chopped

$^1/_2$ jalapeño pepper, seeded and finely chopped

1 teaspoon dried Greek oregano

$^1/_3$ cup nonfat plain yogurt

$^1/_3$ cup nonfat sour cream

$^1/_2$ tomato, chopped

$^1/_2$ red bell pepper, seeded and chopped

2 tablespoons chopped fresh cilantro (see headnote, page 74)

2 scallions, including greens, chopped

Preheat oven to 450 degrees.

Prick potatoes all over with the tines of a fork and place in oven. Bake for about 45 minutes or until tender. Slice top quarter off potatoes and remove flesh from both parts. Discard top skin. Mash flesh with a fork and add remaining ingredients. Divide into four parts and fill skins. Return to oven and cook about 10 minutes or until heated through and golden brown on top.

per serving

Calories	251	Cholesterol	.364 mg
Protein	7.45 g	Calcium	66.6 mg
Carbohydrates	56.2 g	Iron	2.97 mg
Fat—Total	.319 g	Sodium	47.4 mg

herb and garlic stuffed potatoes

Here's another winning potato recipe for your collection.

serves 4

4 Idaho potatoes, scrubbed and patted dry

4 Roasted Garlic cloves (page 20)

1 tablespoon chopped fresh cilantro (see headnote, page 74)

1 tablespoon chopped fresh mint

1 tablespoon chopped fresh basil

1 scallion, including greens, chopped

2 teaspoons Dijon mustard

1 1/2 tablespoons orange juice

1 teaspoon salt

Preheat oven to 450 degrees.

Prick potatoes all over with the tines of a fork and place in oven. Bake for about 45 minutes or until tender. Slice top quarter off potatoes and remove flesh from both parts. Discard top skins. Mash flesh with a fork and add remaining ingredients. Divide into four parts and fill skins. Return to oven and cook about 10 minutes or until heated through and golden brown on top.

per serving

Calories	225	Cholesterol	0 mg
Protein	4.82 g	Calcium	23.6 mg
Carbohydrates	51.7 g	Iron	2.81 mg
Fat—Total	.338 g	Sodium	582 mg

overstuffed watercress potatoes

4 Idaho potatoes, scrubbed and patted dry

1/2 bunch watercress, chopped

3/4 cup nonfat cream cheese

1/4 teaspoon black pepper

1/2 teaspoon salt

2 Roasted Garlic cloves (page 20)

1 1/2 teaspoons Dijon mustard

2 teaspoons chopped fresh dill

Preheat oven to 450 degrees.

Prick potatoes all over with the tines of a fork and place in oven. Bake for about 45 minutes or until tender. Slice top quarter off potatoes and remove flesh from both parts. Discard top skins. Mash flesh with a fork and add remaining ingredients. Divide into four parts and fill skins. Return to oven and cook about 10 minutes or until heated through and golden brown on top.

per serving

Calories	297	Cholesterol	15 mg
Protein	16.9 g	Calcium	29.9 mg
Carbohydrates	54.1 g	Iron	2.8 mg
Fat—Total	.298 g	Sodium	820 mg

garlic roasted radicchio

Tart, sweet, aromatic, garlic roasted radicchio is the perfect first experience for people who haven't yet tried this wonderful, slightly bitter red vegetable.

serves 4

8 garlic cloves, peeled and finely chopped

1 tablespoon finely chopped fresh rosemary or 1 teaspoon dried

$^1/_4$ cup balsamic vinegar

4 heads radicchio, halved through the stems

Preheat oven to 400 degrees.

Combine garlic, rosemary, and balsamic vinegar and pour into a shallow baking pan. Place radicchio halves, cut side down, in the pan. Bake for about 45 minutes or until radicchio is browned and soft.

per serving

Calories	11.3	Cholesterol	0 mg
Protein	.576 g	Calcium	8.5 mg
Carbohydrates	2.68 g	Iron	.316 mg
Fat—Total	.1 g	Sodium	8.95 mg

spinach with oriental flavors

Fresh spinach with a hint of the Orient. For variety, try substituting broccoli rabe for the spinach.

serves 4

1½–2 pounds fresh spinach (weight before stemming), stems trimmed and discarded

1 teaspoon soy sauce

½ teaspoon ground ginger

½ teaspoon garlic powder

1 teaspoon toasted sesame seeds

Salt and pepper to taste

Wash the spinach well and shake out the water. Heat a large saucepan over high heat and add the spinach. Cook for about 5–7 minutes, stirring occasionally, until spinach is wilted. Just before serving, stir in remaining ingredients. Salt and pepper to taste.

per serving

Calories	48.7	Cholesterol	0 mg
Protein	5.88 g	Calcium	204 mg
Carbohydrates	7.25 g	Iron	5.53 mg
Fat—Total	1.07 g	Sodium	242 mg

diet workshop's recipes for healthy living

butternut squash puree

Once you try butternut squash, you'll be hooked. It's sweet, creamy, and thanks to modern science, available just about all year long.

serves 4

1 butternut squash, peeled, seeded, and sliced

1 shallot, peeled and chopped

1 quarter-size slice of fresh gingerroot

2–3 cups Chicken or Vegetable Stock (page 18 or 17), or low-sodium canned or from bouillon cubes

$^1/_2$ teaspoon salt

$^1/_4$ teaspoon ground cardamom

Preheat oven to 450 degrees.

Place butternut squash, shallot, gingerroot, and 1 cup of the chicken stock in a shallow pan and bake for about 1 hour or until the squash is very soft.

Place pan contents in a food processor fitted with a steel blade. Process until smooth, gradually adding chicken stock, salt, and cardamom, or until puree resembles mashed potatoes. Reheat prior to serving if necessary.

per serving

Calories	82.5	Cholesterol	0 mg
Protein	3.85 g	Calcium	69.1 mg
Carbohydrates	17 g	Iron	1.21 mg
Fat—Total	.861 g	Sodium	309 mg

stuffed acorn squash

Fancy enough for a holiday dinner, simple enough for every day.

serves 4

2 cups water

2 acorn squash, halved and seeded

$1/2$ small Spanish onion, peeled and coarsely chopped

$1/2$ Granny Smith apple, peeled, if desired, and diced

I stalk celery, finely diced

I cup fresh or frozen cranberries

2 tablespoons cognac

$1/4$ teaspoon ground cinnamon

$1/2$ teaspoon salt

2 tablespoons chopped walnuts (optional)

I egg white

3 tablespoons apple or orange juice

Preheat oven to 400 degrees.

Pour $1\frac{1}{2}$ cups water into a large shallow baking dish. Add squash, cut side down, and bake for 35 minutes or until squash begins to soften.

While the squash is baking, prepare the filling. Combine onion, apple, and celery in a medium-size pan and cook, over medium-low heat, for 15 minutes or until the apple is soft. Off heat, add remaining ingredients.

Remove squash from oven and let sit until cool enough to handle. Scoop out half of the flesh, leaving enough so the squash retains its shape. Do not break the skin. Add scraped-out squash to apple mixture.

Divide stuffing into 4 parts and fill squashes. Bake for 30 more minutes or until tender.

per serving

Calories	195	Cholesterol	0 mg
Protein	4.11 g	Calcium	105 mg
Carbohydrates	39.8 g	Iron	2.18 mg
Fat—Total	2.81 g	Sodium	298 mg

swiss chard with potatoes

Though you won't see Swiss chard on too many menus in the United States, it's a popular vegetable in Europe. Try this unfamiliar green and you'll wonder why you haven't had it before.

serves 4

6 new potatoes, scrubbed and quartered

I bunch Swiss chard, washed but not dried, woody stems and bottoms discarded, leaves coarsely chopped

$1/2$ teaspoon crushed red pepper flakes (optional)

Salt and pepper

Boil potatoes until tender, set aside.

Heat a nonstick pan over high heat and add the wet Swiss chard. Cook for about 5 minutes or until wilted. Add potatoes and pepper flakes. Salt and pepper to taste.

per serving

Calories	34.9	Cholesterol	0 mg
Protein	1.06 g	Calcium	11.8 mg
Carbohydrates	7.81 g	Iron	.986 mg
Fat—Total	.146 g	Sodium	175 mg

diet workshop's recipes for healthy living

roasted cherry tomatoes

Although the recipe calls for cherry tomatoes, which are particularly sweet and, therefore, good roasted, feel free to substitute your own favorite kind. If you can find yellow cherry tomatoes, combine them with the red, half and half, and your dish will be a delight for the eyes as well as the mouth.

serves 4

Olive oil cooking spray

4 cups cherry tomatoes

1 teaspoon olive oil

$^1/_2$ teaspoon kosher salt

Fresh basil, dill, tarragon, or oregano, chopped (for garnish)

Preheat oven to 400 degrees. Lightly spray a baking sheet with cooking spray.

Place tomatoes on baking sheet and sprinkle with oil and salt. Bake for about 30 minutes or until the tomatoes have browned and popped. Garnish with fresh herbs.

per serving

Calories	38.5	Cholesterol	0 mg
Protein	1.16 g	Calcium	7.11 mg
Carbohydrates	6.31 g	Iron	.617 mg
Fat—Total	1.57 g	Sodium	279 mg

stuffed zucchini

Hearty enough for a meal in itself, stuffed zucchini is a perfect complement to a big green salad.

serves 4

Olive oil cooking spray

4 medium-size zucchini

1 fresh tomato, finely diced

$1/2$ cup bread crumbs or leftover cooked white rice

1 tablespoon dried basil

1 tablespoon grated Parmesan cheese

2 tablespoons crumbled goat cheese

2 teaspoons dried Greek oregano

2 tablespoons pine nuts

2 garlic cloves, peeled and finely chopped

$1/4$ teaspoon black pepper

$1/8$ teaspoon salt

Preheat oven to 400 degrees. Lightly coat a baking pan with cooking spray.

Lay the zucchini on a cutting board and slice off the top quarter lengthwise. Hollow out the bottom and set it aside. Finely chop the insides and the top.

Place the chopped zucchini in a large mixing bowl and add the remaining ingredients. Divide it into four equal parts and stuff into the hollowed-out zucchini shells. Place on baking sheet and bake for about 35–40 minutes or until the zucchini is tender and the top is browned.

per serving

Calories	96.7	Cholesterol	2.63 mg
Protein	4.79 g	Calcium	76.7 mg
Carbohydrates	14.6 g	Iron	1.66 mg
Fat—Total	2.86 g	Sodium	219 mg

roasted mixed vegetables

Long, slow roasting brings out a richness and depth of flavor in these vegetables that can't be achieved with any other method.

serves 4

1 red onion, peeled and sliced

2 red bell peppers, seeded and sliced

1 yellow bell pepper, seeded and sliced

1 yellow squash, sliced diagonally

4 garlic cloves, peeled and chopped

1 teaspoon dried thyme

$^1/_4$ teaspoon kosher salt

$^1/_4$ teaspoon black pepper

2 tablespoons balsamic vinegar

Preheat oven to 400 degrees.

Combine all the ingredients, except for the balsamic vinegar, together in a baking pan, and cook for about 1½ hours or until well browned.

Sprinkle with balsamic vinegar.

Serve hot, cold, or at room temperature.

per serving

Calories	42.7	Cholesterol	0 mg
Protein	1.7 g	Calcium	25.7 mg
Carbohydrates	9.91 g	Iron	.755 mg
Fat—Total	.342 g	Sodium	136 mg

ratatouille

A nonfat version of the classic French vegetable combo.

serves 4

1 small red onion, peeled and chopped

4–5 garlic cloves, peeled and chopped

2 tablespoons water

1 eggplant, peeled and cubed

1 celery stalk, cubed

1 carrot, cubed

1 teaspoon dried basil

1 teaspoon dried Greek oregano

1 (35-ounce) can tomatoes, cut up, including liquid

1 (28-ounce) can chopped tomatoes, including liquid

2 zucchini, cubed

Heat a nonstick skillet over medium heat, add onion, garlic, and water, and cook until the onion is soft, about 5–10 minutes. Reduce heat to medium low, add remaining ingredients, and cook until all the vegetables are soft, about 1 hour.

per serving

Calories	155	Cholesterol	0 mg
Protein	6.61 g	Calcium	150 mg
Carbohydrates	34.2 g	Iron	3.69 mg
Fat—Total	1.59 g	Sodium	749 mg

salads and salad dressings

gazpacho salad with gruyère or baby swiss

This is no ordinary salad; add some French bread and you have a complete meal. Experiment with different cheeses and different fresh herbs; basil is particularly good.

serves 4

dressing:

2 garlic cloves, peeled

$1/8$ – $1/4$ teaspoon cayenne pepper

2 teaspoons dried basil

$1/3$ teaspoon salt

2 tablespoons red wine vinegar

1 tablespoon olive or canola oil

salad:

2 cups cherry tomatoes

$1/2$ bunch scallions, white part thinly sliced, green part coarsely chopped

1 bell pepper, any color, seeded and cubed

2 cucumbers, peeled, seeded, and sliced

$1/2$ cup cubed Gruyère or Baby Swiss cheese

2 tablespoons fresh dill

To make the dressing, place garlic, cayenne, dried basil, and salt in the bowl of a food processor fitted with a steel blade. Process until combined. With the machine still running, gradually add vinegar and then oil.

Arrange tomatoes, scallions, pepper, cucumbers, cheese, and dill in a large serving bowl. Sprinkle with dressing.

per serving

Calories	142	Cholesterol	18.1 mg
Protein	6.93 g	Calcium	202 mg
Carbohydrates	9.94 g	Iron	1.05 mg
Fat—Total	9.18 g	Sodium	243 mg

watercress salad with pears and gorgonzola

The sweetness of the pears and the richness of the Gorgonzola make this oil-free salad a surprisingly rich one.

serves 4

1 bunch watercress, stems removed, if desired

$^1/_2$ head romaine lettuce, torn apart

1 ripe pear, peeled if desired, cored and cubed

2 tablespoons crumbled Gorgonzola cheese

1 tablespoon red wine vinegar

1 tablespoon balsamic vinegar

Arrange watercress, romaine lettuce, and pear in a large salad bowl. Sprinkle with remaining ingredients.

Serve immediately.

per serving

Calories	47	Cholesterol	3.12 mg
Protein	1.91 g	Calcium	49 mg
Carbohydrates	7.83 g	Iron	.643 mg
Fat—Total	1.38 g	Sodium	70.9 mg

fennel and parmesan

1–2 fennel bulbs, thinly sliced, fernlike tips reserved for garnish

1 1/2 × 1 1/2-inch chunk Parmesan cheese, shaved with a potato peeler into thin strips

2 teaspoons olive oil

2–4 tablespoons red wine vinegar

Salt and pepper to taste

Place fennel and Parmesan cheese in a shallow serving bowl and sprinkle with olive oil and vinegar. Add salt and pepper to taste. Garnish with fennel ferns.

per serving

Calories	77.1	Cholesterol	4.92 mg
Protein	3.69 g	Calcium	130 mg
Carbohydrates	7.31 g	Iron	.773 mg
Fat—Total	4.3 g	Sodium	162 mg

mango and tomato with curry and basil

This salad will have special appeal to fans of Indian cuisine.

serves 4

2 tablespoons fresh orange juice

I teaspoon curry powder or to taste

2 mangoes, peeled and cubed

2 fresh tomatoes, cubed

8 fresh basil leaves, julienned

Salt to taste

Combine orange juice and curry powder in a small bowl or glass and set aside.

Arrange mangoes and tomatoes in a large salad bowl. Sprinkle dressing over mangoes and tomatoes and toss lightly. Add basil leaves and salt to taste.

per serving

Calories	83.6	Cholesterol	0 mg
Protein	1.13 g	Calcium	15.8 mg
Carbohydrates	21.3 g	Iron	.459 mg
Fat—Total	.504 g	Sodium	7.74 mg

diet workshop's recipes for healthy living

black bean salad

Southwestern in origin, this salad will liven the meals of any cuisine.

serves 4

5 tablespoons fresh lime juice

5 tablespoons fresh orange juice

$^1/_2$ teaspoon ground cumin

$^1/_2$ teaspoon cayenne pepper

$^1/_2$ teaspoon salt

6 cups cooked black turtle beans (see Note, page 35)

$^1/_4$ cup chopped fresh cilantro (see headnote, page 74)

1 bunch scallions, including greens, chopped

1 red bell pepper, seeded and diced

1 yellow bell pepper, seeded and diced

Combine lime juice, orange juice, cumin, cayenne, and salt in a small bowl and set aside.

Place remaining ingredients in a large serving bowl, mix together and sprinkle with the dressing. Cover and refrigerate at least 4 hours to let the flavors meld.

per serving

Calories	376	Cholesterol	0 mg
Protein	23.9 g	Calcium	89.4 mg
Carbohydrates	69.9 g	Iron	5.94 mg
Fat—Total	1.62 g	Sodium	273 mg

white bean salad with herbes de provence

This high-protein salad is easy and quick to prepare and its flavor is intense and unusual.

serves 4

1 (16-ounce) can white cannellini beans, drained and rinsed with cold water

1 teaspoon herbes de Provence

3 tablespoons balsamic vinegar

2 tablespoons chopped fresh parsley or basil

Combine all the ingredients in a medium-size serving bowl. Cover and refrigerate at least 2 hours.

per serving

Calories	120	Cholesterol	0 mg
Protein	8.3 g	Calcium	79.2 mg
Carbohydrates	22.1 g	Iron	3.26 mg
Fat—Total	.306 g	Sodium	5.25 mg

diet workshop's recipes for healthy living

five-bean salad

Try this salad as a meal in itself or reduce the serving size and serve it with cold grilled chicken and fresh fruit.

serves 4

1 shallot, peeled and chopped

2 garlic cloves, peeled

1/4 cup red wine vinegar

1/4 cup balsamic vinegar

1/2 teaspoon salt

4 tablespoons Dijon mustard

2 teaspoons dried basil

1 cup canned or cooked red kidney beans (see Note, page 35)

1 cup canned or cooked black turtle beans (see Note, page 35)

1 cup canned or cooked white cannellini or kidney beans (see Note, page 35)

1 cup canned or cooked garbanzo beans (see Note, page 35)

2 cups uncooked green beans, trimmed and halved

1/2 bunch scallions, including greens, chopped

1 cup coarsely chopped fresh parsley

Place shallot, garlic cloves, both vinegars, salt, mustard, and basil in the bowl of a food processor fitted with a steel blade. Process until combined and set aside.

Arrange the remaining ingredients in a large serving bowl and sprinkle with the dressing. Cover and refrigerate at least 4 hours.

per main course serving

Calories	293	Cholesterol	0 mg
Protein	18.3 g	Calcium	157 mg
Carbohydrates	53.2 g	Iron	7.46 mg
Fat—Total	2.71 g	Sodium	481 mg

arugula salad with mango

Both sharp and sweet, this salad is a great taste combination, perfect as the first course for a summer meal.

serves 4

I bunch arugula

I head Belgian endive, cut in rounds

I large mango, peeled and diced

I tablespoon olive oil

I tablespoon balsamic vinegar

Salt and pepper to taste

Combine arugula, endive, and mango in a large mixing or salad bowl.

Sprinkle with oil, balsamic vinegar, salt, and pepper.

per serving

Calories	70.4	Cholesterol	0 mg
Protein	.722 g	Calcium	20.3 mg
Carbohydrates	10.3 g	Iron	.367 mg
Fat—Total	3.59 g	Sodium	8.77 mg

diet workshop's recipes for healthy living

cracked wheat with fruit, vegetables, and mint

This slightly exotic flavor-packed salad is a meal in itself.

$^1/_2$ cup medium-grind cracked wheat (bulgar)

$^3/_4$ cup boiling water

1 tablespoon fresh lemon juice

$^1/_4$ cup fresh orange juice

1 cup chopped snow peas

2 scallions, including greens, chopped

$^1/_2$ bunch fresh parsley, chopped

$^1/_4$ cup finely chopped fresh mint

1 red bell pepper, seeded and diced

1 fresh orange, peeled, sectioned, and chopped

$^1/_4$ cup currants

$^1/_2$ teaspoon salt

1 tablespoon olive oil

Place cracked wheat, water, lemon juice, and orange juice in a large bowl. Let sit 10–20 minutes or until the wheat has softened and the liquid has been absorbed. Layer on the remaining ingredients in the order in which they appear. Cover and refrigerate at least 4 hours or overnight. Just prior to serving, mix well.

per serving

Calories	139	Cholesterol	0 mg
Protein	4.04 g	Calcium	46.3 mg
Carbohydrates	24.6 g	Iron	1.52 mg
Fat—Total	3.82 g	Sodium	273 mg

tuscan bread salad

A classic Italian dish, minus the olive oil. The taste of this salad will fool even the most ardent anti-dieter.

serves 4

2 cups cubed day-old French or sourdough bread

2 medium tomatoes, diced

1 cucumber, peeled, seeded, halved, and thinly sliced

1 fresh red, green, or yellow bell pepper, seeded and cubed

$^1/_4$ cup coarsely chopped fresh chives

$^1/_4$ cup coarsely chopped fresh basil

1 tablespoon finely chopped fresh oregano

$^1/_4$ bunch fresh parsley, coarsely chopped

1–2 garlic cloves, peeled and finely chopped or crushed

1 tablespoon red wine vinegar

$^1/_2$ teaspoon salt

$^1/_4$ teaspoon black pepper

Combine bread, vegetables, chives, basil, oregano, and parsley in a large serving bowl.

Place garlic, vinegar, salt, and black pepper in the bowl of a food processor fitted with a steel blade. Process until combined. Pour over vegetables and toss lightly.

per serving

Calories	88.1	Cholesterol	0 mg
Protein	3.13 g	Calcium	32.2 mg
Carbohydrates	17.7 g	Iron	1.14 mg
Fat—Total	.992 g	Sodium	407 mg

mustard potato salad

1½–2 pounds new potatoes (about 10–12), cut into quarters or halves, depending on size and taste

2 tablespoons nonfat plain yogurt

1–2 tablespoons light mayonnaise

2 tablespoons Dijon mustard

2 tablespoons nonfat sour cream

2 celery stalks, julienned

2 carrots, julienned

2 scallions, including greens, chopped

Salt and pepper to taste

Place potatoes in a stockpot and cover with cold water. Bring to a boil over high heat and cook until the potatoes are tender, about 15 minutes. Drain and place in a bowl and set aside to cool to room temperature.

Combine yogurt, mayonnaise, mustard, and sour cream. Pour over potatoes and stir until they are well coated. Add celery, carrots, and scallions and gently mix. Add salt and pepper to taste. Serve cold or at room temperature.

per serving

Calories	239	Cholesterol	2.01 mg
Protein	5.88 g	Calcium	61 mg
Carbohydrates	50.8 g	Iron	2.83 mg
Fat—Total	2.15 g	Sodium	192 mg

greek cucumber salad

This traditional Greek salad is so rich and flavorful it's almost a condiment. Served inside pita bread, it makes a great sandwich; served on the side, it's good with almost anything.

serves 4

4 cucumbers, peeled, halved, seeded, and thinly sliced

1/4 teaspoon salt

2 garlic cloves, peeled and finely chopped or crushed

1/2 cup Yogurt Cheese (page 19)

Pinch black pepper

1 tablespoon finely chopped fresh mint

Place cucumber slices in a colander over a bowl or deep plate and sprinkle with salt. Cover and refrigerate overnight.

The next day, blot the cucumbers dry with a paper towel to rid them of excess salt.

Add remaining ingredients.

per serving

Calories	69.4	Cholesterol	3.15 mg
Protein	5.03 g	Calcium	140 mg
Carbohydrates	11 g	Iron	.812 mg
Fat—Total	1.21 g	Sodium	165 mg

cucumber, red onion, and feta salad

Try this salad packed inside pita bread or serve it with grilled chicken or fish.

4 cucumbers, peeled, seeded, and thinly sliced

$^1/_4$ teaspoon salt

$^1/_2$ red onion, peeled and thinly sliced

$^1/_2$ cup crumbled feta cheese

$^1/_4$ cup chopped fresh mint

$^1/_4$ cup chopped fresh parsley

Place cucumber slices in a colander over a bowl or deep plate and sprinkle with salt. Cover and refrigerate overnight.

The next day, blot the cucumbers dry with a paper towel to rid them of excess salt.

Combine with remaining ingredients and gently toss. Serve at once.

per serving

Calories	126	Cholesterol	27.4 mg
Protein	6.72 g	Calcium	201 mg
Carbohydrates	10.8 g	Iron	1.27 mg
Fat—Total	7.01 g	Sodium	350 mg

salad of mixed greens

The lettuces in this salad are so flavorful, you won't want to mask them with a heavy dressing.

$^1/_2$ bunch watercress, torn into bite-size pieces

$^1/_2$ bunch arugula, torn into bite-size pieces

$^1/_2$ bunch romaine, torn into bite-size pieces

$^1/_2$ head radicchio, coarsely chopped

$^1/_2$ cup coarsely chopped fresh basil

2 stalks celery, peeled and thinly sliced

$^1/_2$ cup crumbled feta cheese

2 tablespoons grated Parmesan cheese

$^1/_4$ cup balsamic vinegar

Combine watercress, lettuces, basil, celery, and feta cheese in a large salad bowl.

Sprinkle with Parmesan cheese and balsamic vinegar and serve.

per serving

Calories	111	Cholesterol	29.8 mg
Protein	6.78 g	Calcium	229 mg
Carbohydrates	4.83 g	Iron	.997 mg
Fat—Total	7.66 g	Sodium	426 mg

diet workshop's recipes for healthy living

pasta fagioli salad

Like the dish for which this salad is named, pasta fagioli salad is a main course. Add some bread and you have a great meal, any time of year.

serves 4

1 can (16-ounce) cannellini beans, drained and rinsed

1 pint cherry tomatoes, quartered

8 ounces dry pasta bow ties, cooked, drained, and cooled

2 scallions, including green and white parts, sliced

3 carrots, thinly sliced

1 large celery stalk, thinly sliced

3 garlic cloves, peeled

2 tablespoons (4 branches) crushed fresh rosemary

2 tablespoons warm water

3 tablespoons red wine vinegar

2 tablespoons balsamic vinegar

Set aside 2 tablespoons of the white beans and 8 cherry tomatoes.

Toss the pasta, vegetables, and beans together in a large bowl.

To make the dressing, place the garlic and rosemary in the bowl of a food processor fitted with a steel blade. Pulse until finely chopped. Add the reserved white beans and tomatoes and blend until slightly chunky. Add the water, red wine vinegar, and balsamic vinegar and process until combined. Pour over the pasta mixture.

per serving

Calories	370	Cholesterol	0 mg
Protein	16.8 g	Calcium	110 mg
Carbohydrates	73.9 g	Iron	6.12 mg
Fat—Total	1.53 g	Sodium	35.3 mg

red cabbage and carrot slaw

Light, flavorful, and surprising, this dish is a great alternative to traditional mayonnaise-laden coleslaw. For an even lighter version, omit the feta cheese.

serves 4 generously

1/2 medium-size head red cabbage, sliced paper thin by hand (about 6–7 cups)

2 large carrots, julienned or grated

1/4 cup crumbled feta cheese

1/4 cup finely chopped fresh dill

1/4 cup fresh lemon juice

Pepper to taste

Combine ingredients in a large serving bowl. Serve immediately.

per serving

Calories	88.2	Cholesterol	13.7 mg
Protein	4.27 g	Calcium	139 mg
Carbohydrates	11.8 g	Iron	.956 mg
Fat—Total	3.67 g	Sodium	204 mg

carrot salad with radicchio and endive

2 heads endive, julienned

1 small head radicchio, julienned

4–6 carrots, julienned

1 teaspoon dried basil or 1 tablespoon finely chopped fresh basil

6 tablespoons balsamic vinegar

1 tablespoon olive oil

Salt and pepper to taste

Place all ingredients in a large serving bowl and gently toss to combine. Serve immediately.

per serving

Calories	82.5	Cholesterol	0 mg
Protein	1.7 g	Calcium	53.5 mg
Carbohydrates	12.5 g	Iron	1.07 mg
Fat—Total	3.67 g	Sodium	44.9 mg

curried chutney chicken salad

Great on a bed of romaine or inside pita, curried chutney chicken salad is a summertime favorite. Be sure to search for interesting, chunky chutney: Wax Orchards cranberry chutney is especially good.

serves 4

salad:

1 1/2–1 3/4 pounds boneless and skinless chicken breasts, trimmed of fat

2 teaspoons curry powder

1 mango or peach, peeled and chopped

2 scallions, including greens, chopped

2 teaspoons chopped fresh cilantro (optional) (see headnote, page 74)

dressing:

1/3 cup Yogurt Cheese (page 19)

2 teaspoons Dijon mustard

6 tablespoons chutney

2 teaspoons curry powder

2 tablespoons balsamic vinegar

2 teaspoons Chicken Stock (page 18) or low-sodium canned or from bouillon cube

Salt to taste

Place chicken and curry in a skillet large enough to hold all the pieces in a single layer. Cover with cold water and bring to a low boil over medium heat. Reduce heat to low and simmer for about 10 minutes or until chicken is cooked all the way through. Refrigerate until cool. When chicken is cool enough to handle, slice it and place in a bowl. Add peach, scallions, and, if desired, cilantro.

To make the dressing, combine yogurt cheese, Dijon mustard, chutney, curry powder, balsamic vinegar, and chicken stock in a medium-size mixing bowl. Add dressing to chicken and mix until just combined. Cover and refrigerate for at least 4 hours. Add salt to taste.

per serving

Calories	268	Cholesterol	101 mg
Protein	42.6 g	Calcium	119 mg
Carbohydrates	16.6 g	Iron	2.39 mg
Fat—Total	3.26 g	Sodium	221 mg

tabbouli

The classic Mediterranean dish, lightened up.

serves 4

1 cup medium-grind cracked wheat (bulgar)

1 cup boiling water

1 bunch fresh parsley, finely chopped by hand

1 small bunch mint, finely chopped by hand

4 scallions, chopped

$^1/_4$ cup fresh lemon juice

1 cucumber, peeled, if desired, seeded, and diced

2 cups cherry tomatoes, halved or quartered

Combine cracked wheat and boiling water in a medium-size serving bowl. Let sit for 10–20 minutes, or until the wheat has softened and the water has been absorbed.

Layer on the remaining ingredients, except the tomatoes, in the order in which they appear. Cover and refrigerate at least 4 hours or overnight.

Just prior to serving, add tomatoes and gently toss.

per serving

Calories	152	Cholesterol	0 mg
Protein	5.83 g	Calcium	43.5 mg
Carbohydrates	34.1 g	Iron	1.95 mg
Fat—Total	.883 g	Sodium	19.2 mg

curried tuna salad with apples

When most people think of tuna salad, they think of mayonnaise. This alternative is light, flavorful, and so good, you'll never miss the old fat-laden stuff.

serves 4

2 cans (6^1/$_2$ ounces each) tuna packed in water, drained and flaked

4 tablespoons nonfat plain yogurt

2 teaspoons curry powder

2 tablespoons Major Grey's chutney

^{1}/$_2$ Granny Smith apple, peeled, if desired, and cut in small dice

1 tablespoon light mayonnaise (optional)

1 tablespoon chopped fresh cilantro (optional) (see headnote, page 74)

Place tuna in a medium-size mixing bowl. In a separate small bowl, combine yogurt, curry powder, chutney, and apple, and, if desired, mayonnaise and cilantro. Pour yogurt mixture over tuna and mix until just combined. Serve chilled or at room temperature.

per serving

Calories	163	Cholesterol	37.3 mg
Protein	24 g	Calcium	38.6 mg
Carbohydrates	9.13 g	Iron	.679 mg
Fat—Total	3.02 g	Sodium	387 mg

tuna salad with dijon mustard and herbs

Although this recipe calls for little bits of different herbs, the result is well worth the chopping.

serves 4

2 cans (6 ¹/₂ ounces each) white tuna packed in water, drained and flaked

¹/₄ cup nonfat plain yogurt

2 tablespoons Dijon mustard

2 teaspoons balsamic vinegar

2 teaspoons chopped fresh parsley

2 teaspoons chopped fresh basil

2 teaspoons chopped fresh chives

Salt and pepper to taste

Place tuna in a medium-size mixing bowl. Mix in remaining ingredients. Serve chilled or at room temperature.

per serving

Calories	132	Cholesterol	36.4 mg
Protein	24.2 g	Calcium	41 mg
Carbohydrates	2.12 g	Iron	.73 mg
Fat—Total	2.5 g	Sodium	447 mg

white bean and tuna salad

This protein-packed salad is Italian in origin and has many variations. For great taste and looks, serve it on a bed of dark, bitter greens, for instance arugula and watercress.

serves 4

2 cans (6^1/$_2$ ounces each) white tuna packed in water, drained and flaked

1 (16 ounce) can cannellini beans, drained and rinsed

^{1}/$_2$ cup fresh lemon juice

^{1}/$_2$ teaspoon crushed red pepper flakes or more, to taste

^{1}/$_2$ small red onion, peeled and chopped

Salt and pepper to taste

In a medium-size mixing bowl combine tuna, cannellini beans, lemon juice, crushed red pepper flakes, and red onion. Salt and pepper to taste. Serve at room temperature.

per serving

Calories	254	Cholesterol	36.1 mg
Protein	32 g	Calcium	89.9 mg
Carbohydrates	26.2 g	Iron	3.91 mg
Fat—Total	2.51 g	Sodium	343 mg

tuna salad with sherry and dill

¹/₄ cup nonfat plain yogurt

1 tablespoon chopped fresh dill

2 teaspoons dry sherry

2 cans (6¹/₂ ounces each) white tuna packed in water, drained

Salt and pepper to taste

Combine yogurt, dill, sherry, and tuna in a medium-size bowl. Salt and pepper to taste. Serve chilled or at room temperature.

per serving

Calories	127	Cholesterol	36.4 mg
Protein	23.8 g	Calcium	34.1 mg
Carbohydrates	1.21 g	Iron	.539 mg
Fat—Total	2.14 g	Sodium	349 mg

balsamic vinaigrette

Double or triple this recipe; this simple dressing is great on all your favorite greens, and it will last in your refrigerator for at least 4 weeks.

yield: about 1 cup

2 garlic cloves, peeled and chopped or sliced

$^1/_2$ teaspoon Dijon mustard

1 teaspoon salt

$^1/_2$ cup balsamic vinegar

$^3/_8$ cup olive oil

$^3/_8$ cup warm water

Place garlic cloves, mustard, and salt in the bowl of a food processor fitted with a steel blade. Process until combined. Add vinegar and process. With the machine still running, add the olive oil and water very gradually, 1 tablespoon at a time.

per 2 tablespoons

Calories	46.5	Cholesterol	0 mg
Protein	.008 g	Calcium	.751 mg
Carbohydrates	.454 g	Iron	.068 mg
Fat—Total	5.14 g	Sodium	135 mg

cucumber dressing

Smooth and cool, this dressing enhances cucumbers, green salads, or even canned tuna.

yield: about 1 cup

1 cucumber, peeled, seeded, and thinly sliced or chopped

¾ cup nonfat plain yogurt

2 garlic cloves, peeled and minced

1 tablespoon red wine vinegar

Combine all ingredients in a bowl.

per 2 tablespoons

Calories	8.95	Cholesterol	.207 mg
Protein	.786 g	Calcium	25.6 mg
Carbohydrates	1.46 g	Iron	.065 mg
Fat—Total	.045 g	Sodium	9.15 mg

basil vinaigrette

The perfect dressing for sliced fresh tomatoes, basil vinaigrette also goes well on mixed greens or cold pasta.

yield: about 1 1/2 cups

1/2 cup red wine vinegar

1/4 cup fresh basil

1/4 cup grainy Dijon mustard

1/2 cup olive oil

1/4 cup warm water

Place vinegar, basil, and mustard in the bowl of a food processor fitted with a steel blade. Process until combined. With the machine still running, add the olive oil and water very gradually, 1 tablespoon at a time.

per 2 tablespoons

Calories	44.3	Cholesterol	0 mg
Protein	.231 g	Calcium	18.3 mg
Carbohydrates	.919 g	Iron	.414 mg
Fat—Total	4.65 g	Sodium	32.9 mg

buttermilk dressing

This show-off dressing for company may turn out to be a family favorite.

yield: about 1 1/2 cups

1 cup skim-milk buttermilk

1/4 cup white vinegar

1 tablespoon fresh tarragon or 1 teaspoon dried French tarragon

1 teaspoon dried thyme

1/4 cup olive oil

Place buttermilk, vinegar, tarragon, and thyme in the bowl of a food processor fitted with a steel blade. Process until combined. With the machine still running, add the olive oil very gradually, 1 tablespoon at a time.

per 2 tablespoons

Calories	24.4	Cholesterol	.358 mg
Protein	.338 g	Calcium	12 mg
Carbohydrates	.635 g	Iron	.029 mg
Fat—Total	2.34 g	Sodium	10.7 mg

chutney yogurt dressing

A great way to make a fruit salad more exciting, chutney yogurt dressing goes particularly well with tropical fruits such as mangoes, papayas, and bananas.

yield: ³/4 cup

³/4 cup nonfat plain yogurt

3 tablespoons chutney

1 teaspoon curry powder (optional)

Combine all ingredients in a bowl.

per 2 tablespoons

Calories	14.9	Cholesterol	.276 mg
Protein	.931 g	Calcium	31.9 mg
Carbohydrates	2.83 g	Iron	.065 mg
Fat—Total	.044 g	Sodium	21.1 mg

chive vinaigrette

You'll find many uses for this vinaigrette, with the added oniony bursts of chives.

yield: about 1 cup

1/2 bunch chives, chopped

2 teaspoons Dijon mustard

1/4 cup red wine vinegar

2 tablespoons balsamic vinegar

1/4 teaspoon salt

1/4 teaspoon black pepper

1/4 cup olive oil

2 tablespoons water

Place all ingredients except for the olive oil and water in the bowl of a food processor fitted with a steel blade. Process until combined. With the machine still running, add the olive oil and water very gradually, 1 tablespoon at a time.

per 2 tablespoons

Calories	31.3	Cholesterol	0 mg
Protein	.055 g	Calcium	1.62 mg
Carbohydrates	.407 g	Iron	.072 mg
Fat—Total	3.41 g	Sodium	41.5 mg

orange basil vinaigrette

Try this unusual dressing variation on the salad accompanying a one-dish dinner to spark it up.

yield: I cup

2 garlic cloves, peeled and minced

1/4 cup chopped fresh basil

1/2 cup fresh orange juice

I tablespoon sherry vinegar

1/2 teaspoon kosher salt

1/4 cup olive oil

Place garlic and basil in the bowl of a food processor fitted with a steel blade. Process until combined. Add orange juice, vinegar, and salt and process. With the machine still running, add the olive oil very gradually, 1 tablespoon at a time.

per tablespoon

Calories	33.5	Cholesterol	0 mg
Protein	.079 g	Calcium	1.94 mg
Carbohydrates	.862 g	Iron	.053 mg
Fat—Total	3.4 g	Sodium	66.7 mg

ginger vinaigrette

Slightly oriental, this dressing goes well with raw vegetables, particularly bell peppers and cucumbers.

2 teaspoons chopped fresh gingerroot

1 tablespoon chopped fresh parsley

2 garlic cloves, peeled and chopped

$^1/_4$ cup red wine vinegar

$^1/_4$ cup orange juice

$^1/_4$ cup olive oil

Place ginger, parsley, garlic, vinegar, and orange juice in the bowl of a food processor fitted with a steel blade. Process until combined. With the machine still running, add the olive oil very gradually, 1 tablespoon at a time.

per 2 tablespoons

Calories	32.2	Cholesterol	0 mg
Protein	.035 g	Calcium	.665 mg
Carbohydrates	.649 g	Iron	.043 mg
Fat—Total	3.39 g	Sodium	.11 mg

lemon vinaigrette

The lemon lover in your life will appreciate this lively dressing.

yield: about 1 cup

1 bunch chives, chopped

1 large shallot, peeled and chopped

1 tablespoon Dijon mustard

$^{1}/_{2}$ cup lemon juice

$^{1}/_{4}$ teaspoon salt

$^{1}/_{2}$ teaspoon black pepper

$^{1}/_{2}$ cup olive oil

Place chives, shallot, mustard, lemon juice, salt, and pepper in the bowl of a food processor fitted with a steel blade. Process until combined. With the machine still running, add the olive oil very gradually, 1 tablespoon at a time.

per 2 tablespoons

Calories	63.6	Cholesterol	0 mg
Protein	.122 g	Calcium	2.1 mg
Carbohydrates	1.04 g	Iron	.07 mg
Fat—Total	6.81 g	Sodium	45.8 mg

mango chutney vinaigrette

While this vinaigrette is used primarily as a dressing for greens, it can also be served as a sauce for grilled or poached chicken or fish.

yield: about I cup

$^1/_4$ cup Major Grey's chutney

3 tablespoons olive oil

$^1/_3$ cup red wine vinegar

2 teaspoons water

2 teaspoons Dijon mustard

$^1/_2$ teaspoon black pepper

Place all the ingredients in the bowl of a food processor fitted with a steel blade. Pulse until combined, but still a bit chunky.

per 2 tablespoons

Calories	30	Cholesterol	0 mg
Protein	.087 g	Calcium	2.25 mg
Carbohydrates	1.99 g	Iron	.103 mg
Fat—Total	2.58 g	Sodium	17.6 mg

melon salsa

Sweet and tangy, this salsa enhances almost any entree you choose to serve it with.

yield: about 1 cup

$^1/_2$ cup packed chopped fresh basil leaves

1 tomato, diced

$^1/_2$ cantaloupe, flesh cut in small dice

1 tablespoon fresh lime juice

$^1/_2$ teaspoon Chinese chili sauce

$^1/_4$ teaspoon salt

Combine all ingredients in a small bowl, cover and refrigerate for at least 1 hour to let the flavors merge.

whole recipe

Calories	130	Cholesterol	0 mg
Protein	4.03 g	Calcium	70.4 mg
Carbohydrates	30.5 g	Iron	1.81 mg
Fat—Total	1.31 g	Sodium	570 mg

tarragon shallot vinaigrette

For a change of pace, try this dressing on vegetables such as raw carrots or cauliflower and on blanched broccoli.

yield: about 1 ¹/₄ cups

1 shallot, peeled and chopped

1 tablespoon dried French tarragon

¹/₄ teaspoon kosher salt

1 tablespoon Dijon mustard

¹/₂ cup red wine vinegar

3 tablespoons water

¹/₂ cup olive oil

Place shallot, tarragon, salt, and mustard in the bowl of a food processor fitted with a steel blade. Process until combined. With the machine still running, add vinegar, water, and oil very gradually, 1 tablespoon at a time.

per 2 tablespoons

Calories	50.2	Cholesterol	0 mg
Protein	.074 g	Calcium	1.61 mg
Carbohydrates	.657 g	Iron	.09 mg
Fat—Total	5.44 g	Sodium	36.7 mg

oregano garlic vinaigrette

This strong, flavorful vinaigrette is great on cold pasta and salads. It even works as a marinade for chicken or fish.

yield: about I cup

1 teaspoon salt

2 garlic cloves, peeled and chopped

2 tablespoons dried Greek oregano

1 teaspoon dried marjoram

$^1/_2$ teaspoon pepper

$^1/_3$ cup red wine vinegar

$^1/_4$ cup water

$^1/_3$ cup olive oil

Place salt, garlic, oregano, marjoram, and pepper in the bowl of a food processor fitted with a steel blade. Process until combined. With the machine still running, add vinegar, water, and olive oil very gradually, 1 tablespoon at a time.

per 2 tablespoons

Calories	41.8	Cholesterol	0 mg
Protein	.062 g	Calcium	9.32 mg
Carbohydrates	.655 g	Iron	.294 mg
Fat—Total	4.51 g	Sodium	133 mg

basil tomato dressing

For a creamy taste without the fat, nothing beats this dressing.

yield: about 1 cup

1 large bunch fresh basil

2 garlic cloves, peeled and chopped

$^3/_4$ cup nonfat cottage cheese

2 tablespoons nonfat plain yogurt

1 fresh tomato, chopped

Place all ingredients in a food processor fitted with a steel blade and pulse until chunky.

per 2 tablespoons

Calories	9.43	Cholesterol	.504 mg
Protein	1.61 g	Calcium	9.74 mg
Carbohydrates	.814 g	Iron	.064 mg
Fat—Total	.033 g	Sodium	41.7 mg

anchovy dressing

With romaine leaves and croutons, anchovy dressing makes a sort of dietetic Caesar salad.

yield: about 1 cup

2 garlic cloves, peeled and sliced

1 tablespoon anchovy paste

$^1/_3$ cup red wine vinegar

$^1/_4$ cup balsamic vinegar

$^1/_4$ cup water

$^1/_3$ cup olive oil

Place garlic and anchovy paste in the bowl of a food processor fitted with a steel blade. Process until combined. With the machine still running, add both vinegars, water, and olive oil very gradually, 1 tablespoon at a time.

per 2 tablespoons

Calories	41.6	Cholesterol	.425 mg
Protein	.145 g	Calcium	1.69 mg
Carbohydrates	.515 g	Iron	.092 mg
Fat—Total	4.5 g	Sodium	18.4 mg

eggs

tomato basil frittata

Olive oil cooking spray

1 medium-size tomato, diced

1/2 green bell pepper, seeded and diced

3 tablespoons chopped fresh basil

2 tablespoons grated Parmesan cheese

3 large eggs, lightly beaten

6 large egg whites, lightly beaten

1 cup nonfat sour cream, ricotta, or Yogurt Cheese (page 19)

2 cups cooked cubed potatoes (1 large)

1 teaspoon salt

1 teaspoon black pepper

1 teaspoon ground nutmeg

Preheat oven to 350 degrees. Lightly coat an 8-inch springform or pie pan with cooking spray.

Combine tomato, green pepper, basil, and Parmesan cheese in a mixing bowl. Stir in remaining ingredients.

Pour into the prepared pan and bake for about 25–35 minutes or until golden and slightly firm.

per serving

Calories	202	Cholesterol	163 mg
Protein	17.4 g	Calcium	93.9 mg
Carbohydrates	21.9 g	Iron	1.47 mg
Fat—Total	5.33 g	Sodium	797 mg

cauliflower frittata

Frittatas are, surprisingly, great food for those watching what they eat. They are perfect for breakfast, lunch, or dinner, may be served hot, cold, or at room temperature, and are protein-packed, easy to make, and nutritious. Serve with sliced tomatoes or a leafy green salad. Great served with Tomato Salsa (page 23).

serves 4

Olive oil cooking spray

$1/4$ cup water or Vegetable Stock (page 17)

1 Spanish or red onion, peeled and thinly sliced

2 garlic cloves, peeled and finely chopped or crushed

1 head cauliflower (about 3 cups with core removed and florets coarsely chopped)

3 large eggs, lightly beaten

6 large egg whites, lightly beaten

1 cup nonfat sour cream, ricotta, or Yogurt Cheese (page 19)

2 cups cooked cubed potatoes (1 large)

1 teaspoon salt

1 teaspoon black pepper

1 teaspoon ground nutmeg

Preheat oven to 350 degrees. Lightly coat an 8-inch springform or pie pan with cooking spray.

Combine water, onion, and garlic in a small saucepan. Cook over medium-low heat until onion is translucent, about 10 minutes. Add cauliflower and cook 10 minutes more, until soft. Cool to room temperature.

Combine remaining ingredients, by hand, in a mixing bowl; add cooled cauliflower mixture.

Pour into the prepared pan and bake for about 25–35 minutes or until golden and slightly firm.

per serving

Calories	201	Cholesterol	159 mg
Protein	16.9 g	Calcium	49.1 mg
Carbohydrates	26 g	Iron	1.63 mg
Fat—Total	4 g	Sodium	730 mg

shiitake mushroom and pepper frittata

If you like to serve all-in-one meals, this frittata is your dish.

serves 4

Olive oil cooking spray

2 tablespoons Chicken Stock (page 18) or low-sodium canned or from bouillon cube

$^1/_2$ pound fresh shiitake mushrooms (about 10), thinly sliced

2–3 garlic cloves, peeled and finely chopped

3 large eggs, lightly beaten

6 large egg whites, lightly beaten

1 red bell pepper, cored, seeded, and diced

1 yellow bell pepper, cored, seeded, and diced

$^1/_2$ bunch scallions, including greens, thinly sliced

2 cups cubed day-old bread (see Note)

$^1/_2$ teaspoon salt

1 teaspoon black pepper

1 tablespoon finely chopped fresh rosemary or 1 teaspoon dried rosemary

$^1/_2$ pound low-fat goat cheese or nonfat cream cheese, cut up into chunks

$^1/_4$ cup skim milk

Preheat oven to 350 degrees. Lightly coat an 8-inch springform or pie pan with cooking spray.

Place chicken stock, shiitake mushrooms, and garlic in a medium-size saucepan and cook for about 8 minutes or until lightly colored.

While the mushrooms are cooking, whisk the eggs together by hand and add the remaining ingredients. Add the mushrooms. Do not overmix.

Pour the mixture into the prepared pan and bake for about 25–35 minutes or until golden and slightly firm.

NOTE:

You may substitute cooked diced potatoes for the bread.

per serving

Calories	247	Cholesterol	169 mg
Protein	22.3 g	Calcium	74.3 mg
Carbohydrates	27.2 g	Iron	1.78 mg
Fat—Total	4.73 g	Sodium	883 mg

desserts

applesauce

Applesauce with a difference. Works well as both a condiment and a dessert.

4 Granny Smith apples, peeled, if desired, cored, and cut into chunks

I cup water

1–2 quarter-size slices fresh gingerroot (optional)

$1/4$ teaspoon ground cinnamon

I tablespoon brown sugar

$1/4$ teaspoon ground nutmeg

$1/4$ teaspoon vanilla extract

I teaspoon fresh lemon juice

Bring apples, water, and gingerroot to a boil in a medium-size saucepan over high heat. Reduce heat to low and cook for about 25 minutes or until apples are tender. Mash apples and add remaining ingredients. If you like your applesauce smooth, whir in food processor or run through food mill. Serve chilled or at room temperature.

per serving

Calories	134	Cholesterol	0 mg
Protein	.403 g	Calcium	16.7 mg
Carbohydrates	34.4 g	Iron	.425 mg
Fat—Total	.763 g	Sodium	.884 mg

poached pears

Poached pears are a great, light dessert, but one that intimidates a lot of people. This version is almost foolproof. You should feel free to use any kind of pear or wine; or try substituting brown sugar or honey for the white sugar.

serves 4

2 cups water

1 cup wine (red or dry white is fine)

1 cup white sugar

Zest of 1 lemon or orange, cut into thin strips

1/2 vanilla bean, halved lengthwise

1 quarter-size slice fresh gingerroot (optional)

4 firm pears such as Comice or Bosc

Place all the ingredients, except for the pears, in a large saucepan and bring to a very low boil over medium heat. Reduce heat to very low and cook until the sugar has dissolved.

Peel the pears and place them, one at a time, in the poaching liquid, making sure the liquid covers the pears completely. If it doesn't, add more water or wine. Cook for about 12 minutes or until the pears are tender. Let cool in the poaching liquid. Remove vanilla bean and gingerroot.

Remove the pears from the pan and boil down the remaining liquid until it begins to thicken. Serve the poaching liquid with the pears.

per serving

Calories	316	Cholesterol	0 mg
Protein	.601 g	Calcium	21.1 mg
Carbohydrates	71.2 g	Iron	.567 mg
Fat—Total	.556 g	Sodium	3.45 mg

gingerbread

Gingerbread on the light side will provide you with a tasty surprise.

Cooking oil spray

2 tablespoons unsalted butter, at room temperature

$1/2$ cup brown sugar

$1/2$ cup molasses

2 egg whites

2 cups all-purpose white flour

1 teaspoon baking soda

1 tablespoon plus 1 teaspoon ground ginger

1 teaspoon ground cinnamon

$1/2$ teaspoon ground nutmeg

$1/2$ teaspoon salt

2 teaspoons vanilla extract

$1/2$ cup brewed coffee

1 cup nonfat plain yogurt

Preheat oven to 350 degrees. Lightly coat an 8-inch-square pan with cooking spray.

Cream together the butter and brown sugar in a medium-size bowl. Slowly add molasses and egg whites and beat for about 2 minutes. Sift together flour, baking soda, ginger, cinnamon, nutmeg, and salt and beat into batter. Add vanilla, coffee, and yogurt and mix until just combined.

Pour the batter into the prepared pan and bake for about 45 minutes or until a cake tester inserted into the middle comes out clean. Let cake rest 10–15 minutes in pan and then remove it. Serve warm or at room temperature.

per serving

Calories	249	Cholesterol	8.32 mg
Protein	5.9 g	Calcium	117 mg
Carbohydrates	49.3 g	Iron	2.64 mg
Fat—Total	3.26 g	Sodium	314 mg

strawberry rhubarb betty

Spring marks the arrival of rhubarb—a wondrous vegetable that is delicious in many guises. You'll be sure to enjoy this low-calorie version of an old-fashioned favorite.

serves 6

Cooking oil spray

4 rhubarb stalks, halved lengthwise and chopped

1 quart strawberries, hulled and stemmed

$^1/_4$ cup white sugar

$^1/_2$ cup instant rolled oats

$^1/_4$ cup all-purpose white flour

2 tablespoons light margarine, at room temperature

1 teaspoon ground cinnamon

$^1/_4$ cup brown sugar or brown sugar substitute

2 tablespoons dry white wine

Preheat oven to 350 degrees. Lightly coat an 8-inch-square baking pan with cooking spray.

Combine rhubarb, strawberries, and sugar in a medium-size saucepan and bring to a low boil over medium heat. Reduce heat to low and simmer for about 15 minutes or until the rhubarb is soft and the sugar has completely dissolved. Place rhubarb mixture in a prepared pan.

Combine rolled oats, flour, margarine, cinnamon, brown sugar, and wine in a medium-size bowl and mix with your hands or two forks until well combined. Do not do this step with a food processor. Sprinkle over rhubarb. Bake for about 35 minutes or until topping begins to brown.

per serving

Calories	179	Cholesterol	0 mg
Protein	2.8 g	Calcium	76.7 mg
Carbohydrates	32.3 g	Iron	1.16 mg
Fat—Total	4.77 g	Sodium	41.4 mg

berry rhubarb compote

This compote is surprisingly versatile; it can be served all year round, using frozen fruit when fresh is not available, and it can be served at any temperature. In addition, you can layer it with slightly sweetened Yogurt Cheese (page 19) to make a parfait.

serves 4

4 cups chopped fresh or frozen rhubarb (about 2 pounds)

2 cups chopped fresh or frozen strawberries

1 cup fresh or frozen raspberries

$^1/_2$ teaspoon vanilla extract

1 teaspoon cornstarch

$^1/_2$ teaspoon grated lemon peel

$^1/_2$ teaspoon grated orange peel

$^1/_8$ teaspoon ground nutmeg

3 tablespoons brown sugar or brown sugar substitute

Combine rhubarb, berries, vanilla, and cornstarch in a medium-size saucepan and cook over medium-high heat until it reaches a very low boil. Reduce heat to low and simmer for about 40 minutes or until rhubarb is soft and mixture has thickened.

Remove from heat and stir in lemon peel, orange peel, nutmeg, and brown sugar. Serve warm or at room temperature.

per serving

Calories	90.4	Cholesterol	0 mg
Protein	1.82 g	Calcium	127 mg
Carbohydrates	21.4 g	Iron	.85 mg
Fat—Total	.68 g	Sodium	8.31 mg

raspberry banana frozen yogurt

Lower in fat and calories, flavor packed, and better than any ice cream, ice milk, or commercial frozen yogurt, homemade frozen yogurt is a special treat.

serves 4

2 slightly overripe bananas, thinly sliced and frozen

2 cups frozen raspberries

1 cup nonfat plain yogurt

Place frozen bananas and raspberries in the bowl of a food processor fitted with a steel blade. Process until smooth. Gradually add yogurt and process until smooth. Serve immediately.

per serving

Calories	116	Cholesterol	1.1 mg
Protein	4.65 g	Calcium	139 mg
Carbohydrates	25.1 g	Iron	.582 mg
Fat—Total	.722 g	Sodium	47.3 mg

diet workshop's recipes for healthy living

sweet potato chocolate cake

Chocolate cake is always a treat. This version, rich in beta carotene, is specially for dieters and people who choose healthy eating.

serves 9

Cooking oil spray

1 small sweet potato, peeled, if desired, and cubed

$^1/_2$ cup brown sugar

2 large egg whites

$^3/_4$ cup unsweetened cocoa powder

$^1/_4$ cup nonfat plain yogurt

1 cup all-purpose white flour

1 teaspoon baking powder

$^1/_2$ teaspoon baking soda

$^1/_4$ teaspoon salt

Preheat oven to 350 degrees. Lightly coat an 8-inch-square baking pan with cooking spray.

In a small saucepan, cover sweet potato with water and bring to a boil. Puree and reserve 1 cup. Discard the rest or save for another use.

Combine reserved sweet potato with brown sugar, egg whites, and cocoa and beat for 3 minutes or until combined and fluffy. Beat in nonfat yogurt until incorporated.

Sift together flour, baking powder, baking soda, and salt and mix into other ingredients until just combined. Pour into pan and bake for about 35 minutes or until a tester comes out clean.

per serving

Calories	141	Cholesterol	.266 mg
Protein	4.6 g	Calcium	78.1 mg
Carbohydrates	29.8 g	Iron	2.39 mg
Fat—Total	1.98 g	Sodium	209 mg

peach and blueberry cobbler

Cobblers are comfort food: homey, juicy, and warm. By substituting skim milk for the butter and whole milk in the traditional recipes, you eliminate the fat but let the great flavors remain. For variety, substitute strawberries for the blueberries, or nectarines or pears for the peaches.

serves 8

6 ripe peaches, pitted, quartered, and thinly sliced

2 cups blueberries

topping:

$^1/_2$ cup yellow or white cornmeal

$^2/_3$ cup all-purpose white flour

1 teaspoon baking powder

$^1/_4$ teaspoon salt

1 tablespoon white sugar

1 teaspoon grated fresh lemon peel

$^1/_2$ cup skim milk

Preheat oven to 375 degrees.

Combine peaches and blueberries in an 8×8-inch baking pan.

To make the topping, mix cornmeal, flour, baking powder, salt, sugar, and lemon peel in a medium-size bowl until well blended. Gradually stir in skim milk, just until the mixture is moistened. It should remain lumpy.

Spoon dollops of topping over the fruit. Bake for about 25 minutes or until the topping is golden brown.

Let sit 10 minutes before serving.

per serving

Calories	125	Cholesterol	.276 mg
Protein	2.91 g	Calcium	72.4 mg
Carbohydrates	28.5 g	Iron	.953 mg
Fat—Total	.599 g	Sodium	129 mg

ricotta cake with hazelnuts and lemon

Although this recipe has fewer calories and fat than its prototype, cheesecake, it's not a dessert for everyday eating. Save it for a special occasion.

serves 8

$1/2$ cup hazelnuts

1 pound skim-milk ricotta cheese

4 egg yolks

1 teaspoon finely chopped fresh lemon peel

$1/4$ cup white sugar

$1/8$ teaspoon ground nutmeg

$1/2$ teaspoon vanilla extract

Preheat oven to 325 degrees.

Put the hazelnuts on a baking sheet and bake for about 8–10 minutes or until the skins pop. Remove from oven and rub off and discard skins. Grind nuts in a food processor fitted with a steel blade.

Line the bottom of a 7- or 8-inch cake pan with $1/4$ cup of the hazelnuts.

In a food processor fitted with a steel blade, combine the remaining hazelnuts with the other ingredients until smooth. Pour the mixture into the prepared pan and bake for about 25 minutes or until it is slightly golden and tiny bubbles start to appear on the surface. Be careful not to overbake.

Remove the cake from oven and let it sit about 10 minutes or until it starts to pull away from the sides of the pan.

Cool to room temperature, and serve immediately, or refrigerate and serve chilled.

per serving

Calories	185	Cholesterol	123 mg
Protein	8.94 g	Calcium	181 mg
Carbohydrates	10.6 g	Iron	.821 mg
Fat—Total	12.3 g	Sodium	74.2 mg

diet workshop's recipes for healthy living

cranberry apple crisp

Apple crisp, a traditional favorite, takes on a partner and each serves the other well in this tangy and healthy dessert.

serves 8

crust and topping:

$^1/_2$ cup brown sugar

$^3/_4$ cup instant rolled oats

$^3/_4$ cup all-purpose white flour

$^1/_4$ cup butter or margarine, melted

$^1/_4$ cup water

1 teaspoon ground cinnamon

filling:

3 cups fresh or frozen cranberries

2 Granny Smith apples, peeled if desired, and diced

$^1/_4$ cup white sugar

Preheat oven to 350 degrees.

To make the crust and topping, mix the first six ingredients in a large mixing bowl with your hands or two forks until they are well combined. Do not do this step with a food processor. Line the bottom of an 8-inch-square baking pan with half the mixture.

To make the filling, combine cranberries, apples, and sugar in a small mixing bowl. Place on top of crust in pan. Top with remaining oat mixture and bake for about 35 minutes or until golden. Serve hot, chilled, or at room temperature.

per serving

Calories	230	Cholesterol	0 mg
Protein	2.72 g	Calcium	21.5 mg
Carbohydrates	41.7 g	Iron	1.21 mg
Fat—Total	6.57 g	Sodium	56.9 mg

baked apples

1 tablespoon brown sugar or brown sugar substitute

$^1/_2$ teaspoon ground cinnamon

2 tablespoons raisins

1–2 teaspoons grated lemon peel

4 Granny Smith apples, cored and top third cut off and discarded

6 tablespoons dry white wine

Preheat oven to 375 degrees.

Combine brown sugar, cinnamon, raisins, and lemon peel in a small bowl. Divide mixture into four parts and stuff into apples. Arrange apples in a small baking dish so that they touch each other and pour wine around them.

Bake for about 1 hour, or until apples are soft. Serve hot, chilled, or at room temperature.

per serving

Calories	162	Cholesterol	0 mg
Protein	.571 g	Calcium	20.9 mg
Carbohydrates	38.1 g	Iron	.591 mg
Fat—Total	.784 g	Sodium	2.53 mg

baked grapefruit

This dish transforms the grapefruit into an elegant dessert.

2 grapefruits, halved

2 teaspoons white or brown sugar or sugar substitute

8 fresh mint leaves (for garnish)

Preheat broiler.

Place grapefruit halves, cut side up, on a baking sheet and sprinkle with sugar. Broil 5 minutes or until browned and bubbly. Turn broiler off and let sit for 5 minutes in the oven.

Garnish with fresh mint.

per $^1/_2$ grapefruit

Calories	47	Cholesterol	0 mg
Protein	.814 g	Calcium	14.2 mg
Carbohydrates	12 g	Iron	.072 mg
Fat—Total	.118 g	Sodium	.021 mg

chocolate risotto pudding

This pudding is so rich, it's almost impossible to believe it's not loaded with butter and cream. In fact, it's so rich, it's hard to finish what looks like a meager serving.

serves 8

1 cup uncooked Arborio rice (there is no substitute)

4 cups boiling water

$^{1}/_{4}$ cup granulated sugar

$^{1}/_{4}$ cup unsweetened cocoa powder

$^{3}/_{4}$ teaspoon vanilla extract

$^{3}/_{4}$ cup evaporated skim milk

1 tablespoon Grand Marnier

$^{1}/_{4}$ teaspoon ground nutmeg

$^{1}/_{4}$ teaspoon ground cinnamon

Fresh mint leaves (for garnish)

Cook rice and $^{1}/_{2}$ cup boiling water in a saucepan over low heat, stirring constantly, until water is absorbed, about 3 minutes.

Continue adding the water, $^{1}/_{2}$ cup at a time, until it has all been absorbed. This will take about 20 minutes.

Remove from heat and stir in remaining ingredients, except mint, one at a time. Serve warm or chilled, garnished with fresh mint.

per serving

Calories	116	Cholesterol	.861 mg
Protein	3.99 g	Calcium	79 mg
Carbohydrates	23.4 g	Iron	1.44 mg
Fat—Total	.575 g	Sodium	29.3 mg

banana bread

Banana bread, lightened up, is great for breakfast or afternoon tea.

Cooking oil spray

4 slightly overripe, medium-size bananas, mashed

$1/4$ cup margarine, melted

2 eggs

$1 1/2$ teaspoons vanilla extract

$1/2$ cup brown sugar or brown sugar substitute

$3/4$ cup whole wheat flour

$3/4$ cup plus 2 tablespoons all-purpose white flour

2 tablespoons wheat germ

1 teaspoon baking soda

$1/4$ teaspoon salt

$1/2$ teaspoon ground nutmeg

Preheat oven to 350 degrees. Lightly coat an 8-inch loaf pan with cooking spray.

Mix together bananas, margarine, eggs, vanilla extract, and brown sugar in a large mixing bowl until thoroughly combined.

Stir in remaining ingredients until combined. Pour into the prepared loaf pan and bake for about 50 minutes or until golden on top.

per slice

Calories	167	Cholesterol	35.3 mg
Protein	3.78 g	Calcium	17.2 mg
Carbohydrates	27.9 g	Iron	1.17 mg
Fat—Total	5.18 g	Sodium	162 mg

drinks

apple banana smoothie

A meal in a glass—great for breakfast, as a cold soup, or as an afternoon pick-me-up.

yield: 4 cups

1 slightly overripe banana, sliced

1 Granny Smith apple, peeled, if desired, cored, and chopped

1 cup nonfat plain yogurt

$^1/_4$ teaspoon vanilla extract

$^1/_4$ teaspoon ground nutmeg

4 ice cubes

1 cup orange juice

2 tablespoons wheat germ (optional)

Place banana and apple in bowl of food processor fitted with a steel blade. Process until smooth.

Add yogurt, vanilla, nutmeg, and ice cubes and process until smooth.

While machine is running, gradually add orange juice and, if desired, wheat germ.

per 1-cup serving

Calories	132	Cholesterol	1.1 mg
Protein	5.42 g	Calcium	135 mg
Carbohydrates	27.4 g	Iron	.667 mg
Fat—Total	.984 g	Sodium	47.8 mg

tangerine smoothie

Just the thing to cool you down on hot days.

serves 4

1 ¹/₂ cups nonfat vanilla yogurt

¹/₂ cup water

¹/₂ cup pineapple juice

1 tangerine, peeled, seeded, and sectioned

¹/₄ teaspoon ground cinnamon

Place all ingredients in a blender or food processor fitted with a steel blade, and blend until frothy.

per serving

Calories	110	Cholesterol	1.48 mg
Protein	4.92 g	Calcium	172 mg
Carbohydrates	22.7 g	Iron	.186 mg
Fat—Total	.213 g	Sodium	63.5 mg

peach mango smoothie

This fruit-based cooler has great taste and is full of vitamin C.

serves 4

2¹/₂ cups orange juice

1 mango, peeled and sliced

1 slightly overripe banana, sliced

1 peach, sliced

1 teaspoon vanilla extract

Place all ingredients in a blender or food processor fitted with a steel blade and blend until frothy.

per serving

Calories	137	Cholesterol	0 mg
Protein	1.95 g	Calcium	23.5 mg
Carbohydrates	33.5 g	Iron	.444 mg
Fat—Total	.716 g	Sodium	2.88 mg

chocolate banana milkshake

Banana and chocolate combine for an incredibly rich-tasting pick-me-up.

serves 4

2 cups skim milk

2 slightly overripe bananas, sliced

$1/4$ cup chocolate syrup

1 teaspoon vanilla extract

Place all ingredients in a blender or food processor fitted with a steel blade and mix until frothy.

per serving

Calories	136	Cholesterol	2.2 mg
Protein	5.12 g	Calcium	157 mg
Carbohydrates	30.3 g	Iron	.621 mg
Fat—Total	.663 g	Sodium	81.6 mg

Index

Acorn squash, stuffed, 186-87
Amounts and equivalents, 11-13
Anchovies
    with asparagus, garlic, and lemon, 161
    broccoli with, 164
    salad dressing, 233
Apple juice, in rosemary pork chops, 131
Apples
    baked, 256
    crisp, with cranberries, 255
    in curried tuna salad, 215
    smoothie, with banana, 263
Applesauce, 245
Arctic char with sambuca, 81
Artichokes
    pasta with
        and mushrooms, 146
        and tomato, shrimp, and feta cheese, 147
    risotto, 154
Arugula
    as bed for bean and tuna salad, 217
    salad with mango, 202
Asparagus
    amounts and equivalents for, 13
    with anchovies, garlic, and lemon, 161
    with shallots, 162

Baby Swiss cheese, gazpacho salad with, 195
Balsamic onions, 172
Balsamic steak, 120
Balsamic vinaigrette, 219
Banana
    bread, 259
    frozen yogurt, with raspberries, 250
    milkshake, chocolate, 266
    smoothie, with apple, 263
Barbecue
    chicken, Chinese, 85
    sauce, 50
        in mix-ins for burgers, 116
        See also Chipotle barbecue sauce
Basil
    chicken breasts with, and chipotle sauce, 89

in frittata, with tomatoes, 237
in mango-tomato salad with curry, 198
in mix-ins for burgers, 116
in orange steak, 123
in pasta with fresh tomatoes, 148
salad dressing, with tomato, 232
tuna with roasted pepper and, 72
vinaigrette, 221
    with orange, 225
Beans
    amounts and equivalents for, 13
    black
        salad, 199
        soup, 32
    cannellini
        in pasta fagioli, 144-45
        in pasta fagioli salad, 209
        in tuna salad, 217
    five-bean salad, 201
    white
        pasta with broccoli rabe and, 149
        salad, with herbes de Provence, 200
        soup, 34-35
        in tuna salad, 217
Beef
    burgers, mix-ins for, 116-17
    steak, 118-23
        balsamic, 120
        lemon, 118
        orange basil, 123
        with peach and tomato chutney, 90
        southwestern, 121
        spice-rubbed, 119
        three-peppered, 122
    stew, 113
Beets
    amounts and equivalents for, 13
    in borscht, 30
    roasted, 163
Blueberry cobbler, with peaches, 252-53
Bluefish, mustard, 80
Bolognese sauce, pasta with, 142-43
Borscht, chilled, 30
Bread
    banana, 259

gingerbread, 247
salad, Tuscan, 204
Broccoli
    amounts and equivalents for, 13
    anchovies with, 164
    oriental pork with, 126-27
    in overstuffed potatoes, with ricotta cheese, 178
    pasta with, and sun-dried tomatoes, 139
    rabe
        with oriental flavors, 184
        pasta and white beans with, 149
    soup, with other vegetables, 37
Brussels sprouts, spicy, 165
Bulgar. See Cracked wheat
Burgers, mix-ins for, 116-17
Buttermilk dressing, 222
Butternut squash
    amounts and equivalents for, 13
    puree, 185
    soup with sage, 42
    whole roast chicken with, and pears, 104

Cabbage
    amounts and equivalents for, 13
    Chinese, 166
    red, in slaw with carrots, 210
Cajun catfish with fresh watercress sauce, 68-69
Cakes
    chocolate sweet potato, 251
    ricotta, with hazelnuts and lemon, 254
Canadian bacon, in pasta fagioli, 144-45
Cantaloupe salsa, 229
Cardamom, in carrots with ginger, 167
Carmelized onions, 22
    in onion dip, 56
Carrots
    amounts and equivalents for, 13
    with ginger, 167
    salad, with radicchio and endive, 211
    in slaw with red cabbage, 210
    soup, with roasted chestnuts, 43
Catfish, Cajun, with fresh watercress sauce, 68-69

French fries with lemon and garlic, 174

Frittatas. *See* Eggs frittata

Garlic
    amounts and equivalents for, 13
    with asparagus, anchovies, and lemon, 161
    in baked pasta with eggplant sauce, 140-41
    french fries with lemon and, 174
    in linguine with spinach, 150
    pork loin with ginger and, 125
    potatoes with
        herb stuffed, 181
        mashed, 175
    roasted, 20
    in roasted radicchio, 183
    in spicy shrimp, 76
    in veal saltimbocca, 134
    vinaigrette, with garlic, 231

Gazpacho, 27
    salad, with Gruyère or Baby Swiss, 195

Ginger
    carrots with, 167
    marinade, for citrus salmon, 64-65
    pork loin with garlic and, 125
    shrimp, oriental, 79
    in spinach, 184
    vinaigrette, 226

Gingerbread, 247

Gorgonzola cheese in watercress salad, with pears, 196

Grapefruit, baked, 257

Greek cucumber salad, 206

Gruyère cheese, gazpacho salad with, 195

Hazelnuts, in ricotta cake with lemon, 254

Herbes de Provence, white bean salad with, 200

Herbs
    cheese, 52
    chicken with
        quickest, 99
        ricotta and, 100
        thighs with lemon zest and mint, 105
    in linguine giovanni, 151
    in orange salmon, 61
    in pantry supply, 3-4
    in stuffed potatoes with garlic, 181

in tuna salad with mustard, 216
    See also specific herbs

Hoisin sauce, eggplant and peppers in, 170

Honey dip, curried, 54

Honey-glazed chicken breasts with thyme, 87

Ketchup, in mix-ins for burgers, 117

Kitchen, equipping a, 7-10

Lasagna, 152

Leeks, amounts and equivalents for, 13

Lemons, lemon juice, and lemon zest,
    in asparagus with anchovies and garlic, 161
    garlic french fries, 174
    herbed chicken thighs with, and mint, 105
    in ricotta cake with hazelnuts, 254
    sage and, in chicken breasts, 94
    steak, 118
    tarragon and
        chicken breasts, 93
        grilled crabs, 66
    vinaigrette, 227

Limes and lime juice
    in grilled corn with curry, 168
    in marinade for salmon, 64-65

Linguine
    giovanni, 151
    with spinach and garlic, 150

Mangoes
    in argula salad, 202
    chutney vinaigrette, 228
    smoothie, with peach, 265
    in tomato salad, with curry and basil, 198

Marinades
    for chicken
        BBQ, 85
        Marbella, 98
        tandoori, 91
    for salmon, 61, 64-65
    for softshell crabs, 66
    for steak
        lemon steak, 118
        spice-rubbed flank steak, 119

Meat, classic sauce for, 49

Meatballs and spaghetti, 114-15

Melon salsa, 229

Milkshake, chocolate banana, 266

Minestrone, 39, 40-41

Mint
    chicken breasts with, and cilantro, 106-7
    in cracked wheat salad, 203
    herbed chicken thighs with, and lemon zest, 105
    in tabbouli, 214

Mixed greens salad, 208

Mix-ins for burgers, 116-17

Mozzarella cheese, in pizza with roasted vegetables, 156

Mushrooms
    amounts and equivalents for, 13
    pasta with, and artichokes, 146
    soup, double, 36
    wild, trio of, 171

Mussels, pasta with tomatoes and, 138

Mustard
    bluefish, 80
    dip, 55
    in mix-ins for burgers, 116
    oregano pork loin, 128
    pork chops, with orange, 124
    potato salad, 205
    sauce, dilled, 71
    in tuna salad with herbs, 216
    veal chops, 132

Onions
    balsamic, 172
    dip, 58
    in mix-ins for burgers, 117
    red potatoes with fennel and, 177
    See Red onions; Scallions; Spanish onions

Oranges, orange juice, or orange zest
    chicken breasts with red onions and, 96
    in cracked wheat salad, 203
    in herb salmon, 61
    in marinade for salmon, 64–65
    in mustard pork chops, 124
    in risotto, with fennel, 153
    in shrimp with fennel, 77
    spicy shrimp with garlic and glaze of, 76
    in steak with basil, 123
    vinaigrette, with basil, 225

Oregano
    garlic vinaigrette, 231
    in mustard pork loin, 128